AKBAR : BIOGRAPHY OF MUGHAL EMPEROR

BEST BOOKS ON MUGHAL HISTORY FOR UPSC, PSC, CUET

INFO EDGE

Created and Published by

Info Edge

Contents

Foreword

The Info Edge Publication is a unique initiative for sake of reviving books. It was founded on the 29th of December 2021, by Arin Kumar Shukla FRAS and Anant Kumar Shukla. The aim of Info Edge is to provide the best content to the readers and also at the most affordable price. We believe that everyone has the right to knowledge. Currently, Info Edge Publication is selling in 13 countries around the globe.

Acknowledgements

Special thanks to our founders Arin Kumar Shukla FRAS and Anant Kumar Shukla for their effort and commitment to better and affordable knowledge.

KNOW AKBAR

Jalal-ud-din Muhammad Akbar

Abu'l-Fath Jalal-ud-din Muhammad Akbar[8] (25 October 1542[a] – 27 October 1605),[11][12][13] popularly known as Akbar the Great[14] (Persian pronunciation: [akbarı azam]), and also as Akbar I (Persian pronunciation: [akbar]),[15] was the third Mughal emperor, who reigned from 1556 to 1605. Akbar succeeded his father, Humayun, under a regent, Bairam Khan, who helped the young emperor expand and consolidate Mughal domains in India.

With a strong personality and a successful general, Akbar gradually enlarged the Mughal Empire to include much of the Indian subcontinent. His power and influence, however, extended over the entire subcontinent because of Mughal military, political, cultural, and economic dominance. To unify the vast Mughal state, Akbar established a centralized system of administration throughout his empire and adopted a policy of conciliating conquered rulers through marriage and diplomacy. To preserve peace and order in a religiously and culturally diverse empire, he adopted policies that won him the support of his non-Muslim subjects. Eschewing tribal bonds and Islamic state identity, Akbar strove to unite far-flung lands of his realm through loyalty, expressed through an Indo-Persian culture, to himself as an emperor.

Mughal India developed a strong and stable economy, leading to commercial expansion and greater patronage of culture. Akbar himself was a patron of art and culture. He was fond of literature and created a library of over 24,000 volumes written in Sanskrit, Urdu, Persian, Greek, Latin, Arabic, and Kashmiri, staffed by many scholars, translators, artists, calligraphers, scribes, bookbinders, and readers. He did much of the cataloging himself through three main groupings.[16] Akbar also established the library of Fatehpur Sikri exclusively for women,[17] and he decreed that schools for the education of both Muslims and Hindus should be established throughout the realm. He also encouraged bookbinding to become high art.[16] Holy men of many faiths, poets, architects, and artisans adorned his court from all over the world for study and discussion. Akbar's courts at Delhi, Agra, and Fatehpur Sikri became centers of the arts, letters, and learning. Timurid and Perso-Islamic culture began to merge and blend with indigenous Indian elements, and a distinct Indo-Persian culture emerged characterized by Mughal style arts, painting, and architecture. Disillusioned with orthodox Islam and perhaps hoping to bring about religious unity within his empire, Akbar promulgated Din-i-Ilahi, a syncretic creed derived mainly from Islam and Hinduism as well as some parts of Zoroastrianism and Christianity.

Akbar's reign significantly influenced the course of Indian history. During his rule, the Mughal Empire tripled in size and wealth. He created a powerful military system and instituted effective political and social reforms. By abolishing the sectarian tax on non-Muslims and appointing them to high civil and military posts, he was the first Mughal ruler to win the trust and loyalty of the native subjects. He had Sanskrit literature translated, and participated in native festivals, realizing that a stable empire depended on the cooperation and goodwill of his subjects. Thus, the foundations for a multicultural empire under Mughal rule were laid during his reign. Akbar was succeeded as emperor by his son, Prince Salim, later known as Jahangir.

CHAPTER TWO

EARLY YEARS

Akbar as a boy

Defeated in battles at Chausa and Kannauj from 1539 to 1541 by the forces of Sher Shah Suri, Mughal emperor Humayun fled westward to Sindh.[18] There he met and married the then 14-year-old Hamida Banu Begum, daughter of Shaikh Ali Akbar Jami, a Persian teacher of Humayun's younger brother Hindal Mirza. Jalal ud-din Muhammad Akbar was born the next year on 25 October 1542[a] (the fifth day of Rajab, 949 AH)[12] at the Rajput Fortress of Amarkot in Rajputana (in modern-day Sindh), where his parents had been given refuge by the local Hindu ruler Rana Prasad.[20]

During the extended period of Humayun's exile, Akbar was brought up in Kabul by the extended family of his paternal uncles, Kamran Mirza and Askari Mirza, and his aunts, in particular Kamran Mirza's wife. He spent his youth learning to hunt, run, and fight, making him a daring, powerful, and brave warrior, but he never learned to read or write. This, however, did not hinder his search for knowledge as it is always said when he retired in the evening he would have someone read.[21][22] On 20 November 1551, Humayun's youngest brother, Hindal Mirza, died fighting in a battle against Kamran Mirza's forces. Upon hearing the news of his brother's death, Humayun was overwhelmed with grief.[23]

About the time of nine-year-old Akbar's first appointment, as governor of Ghazni, he married Hindal's daughter, Ruqaiya Sultan Begum.[24] Humayun conferred on the imperial couple all the wealth, army, and adherents of Hindal and Ghazni. One of Hindal's jagir was given to his nephew, Akbar, who was appointed as its viceroy and was also given the command of his uncle's army.[25] Akbar's marriage with Ruqaiya was solemnized in Jalandhar, Punjab when both of them were 14-years-old.[26] She was his first wife and chief consort.[27][4]

Following the chaos over the succession of Sher Shah Suri's son Islam Shah, Humayun reconquered Delhi in 1555,[28] leading an army partly provided by his Persian ally Tahmasp I. A few months later, Humayun died. Akbar's guardian, Bairam Khan concealed the death to prepare for Akbar's succession. Akbar succeeded Humayun on 14 February 1556,[29] while amid a war against Sikandar Shah to reclaim the Mughal throne. In Kalanaur, Punjab, the 14-year-old Akbar was enthroned by Bairam Khan on a newly constructed platform, which still stands.[30][31] He was proclaimed Shahanshah (Persian for "King of Kings").[29] Bairam Khan ruled on his behalf until he came of age.[32]

CHAPTER THREE

MILITARY CAMPAIGNS

Mughal Empire under Akbar's period

Akbar was accorded the epithet "the Great" because of his many accomplishments,[33] including his record of unbeaten military campaigns that consolidated Mughal rule in the Indian subcontinent.[29] The basis of this military prowess and authority was Akbar's skillful structural and organizational calibration of the Mughal army.[34] The Mansabdari system in particular has been acclaimed for its role in upholding Mughal power in the time of Akbar. The system persisted with few changes down to the end of the Mughal Empire but was progressively weakened under his successors.[34]

Organizational reforms were accompanied by innovations in cannons, fortifications, and the use of elephants.[33] Akbar also took an interest in matchlocks and effectively employed them during various conflicts. He sought the help of the Ottomans, and also increase of Europeans, especially Portuguese and Italians, in procuring firearms and artillery.[35] Mughal firearms in the time of Akbar came to be far superior to anything that could be deployed by regional rulers, tributaries, or by zamindars.[36] Such was the impact of these weapons that Akbar's Vizier, Abul Fazl, once declared that "except Turkey, there is perhaps no country in which its guns has more means of securing the Government than [India]."[37] The term "gunpowder empire" has thus often been used by scholars and historians in analyzing the success of the Mughals in India. Mughal power has been seen as owing to their mastery of the techniques of warfare, especially the use of firearms encouraged by Akbar.[38]

**Mughal Emperor Akbar training an elephant**

Akbar's father Humayun had regained control of the Punjab, Delhi, and Agra with Safavid support, but even in these areas Mughal rule was precarious, and when the Spurs reconquered Agra and Delhi following the death of Humayun, the fate of the boy emperor seemed uncertain. Akbar's minority and the lack of any possibility of military assistance from the Mughal stronghold of Kabul, which was in the throes of an invasion by the ruler of Badakhshan Prince Mirza Suleiman, aggravated the situation.[39] When his regent, Bairam Khan, called a council of war to marshall the Mughal forces, none of Akbar's chieftains approved. Bairam Khan was ultimately able to prevail over the nobles, however, and it was decided that the Mughals would march against the strongest of the Sur rulers, Sikandar Shah Suri, in Punjab. Delhi was left under the regency of Tardi Baig Khan.[39] Sikandar Shah Suri, however, presented no major concern for Akbar,[40] and avoided giving battle as the Mughal army approached.[citation needed] The gravest threat came from Hemu, a minister and general of one of the Sur rulers, who had proclaimed himself a Hindu emperor and expelled the Mughals from the Indo-Gangetic plains.[39]

Urged by Bairam Khan, who re-marshaled the Mughal army before Hemu could consolidate his position, Akbar marched on Delhi to reclaim it.[41] His army, led by Bairam Khan, defeated Hemu and the Sur army on 5 November 1556 at the Second Battle of Panipat, 50 miles (80 km) north of Delhi.[42] Soon after the battle, Mughal forces occupied Delhi and then Agra. Akbar made a triumphant entry into Delhi, where he stayed for a month. Then he and Bairam Khan returned to Punjab to deal with Sikandar Shah, who had become active again.[43] In the next six months, the Mughals won another major battle against Sikander Shah Suri, who fled east to Bengal. Akbar and his forces occupied Lahore and then seized Multan in Punjab. In 1558, Akbar took possession of Ajmer, the aperture to Rajputana, after the defeat and flight of its Muslim ruler.[43] The Mughals had also besieged and defeated the Sur forces in control of Gwalior Fort, the greatest stronghold north of the Narmada river.[43]

Royal begums, along with the families of Mughal amirs, were finally brought over from Kabul to India at the time – according to Akbar's vizier, Abul Fazl, "so that men might become settled and be restrained in some measure from departing to a country to which they were accustomed".[39] Akbar had firmly declared his intentions that the Mughals were in India to stay. This was a far cry from the political settlements of his grandfather, Babur, and father, Humayun, both of whom had done little to indicate that they were anything but transient rulers.[39][43] However, Akbar methodically re-introduced a historical legacy of the Timurid Renaissance that his ancestors had left.[44]

Akbar hawking with Mughal chieftains and noblemen accompanied by his guardian Bairam Khan

By 1559, the Mughals had launched a drive to the south into Rajputana and Malwa.[45] However, Akbar's disputes with his regent, Bairam Khan, temporarily put an end to the expansion.[45] The young emperor, at the age of eighteen, wanted to take a more active part in managing affairs. Urged on by his foster mother, Maham Anga, and his relatives, Akbar decided to dispense with the services of Bairam Khan. After yet another dispute in court, Akbar finally dismissed Bairam Khan in the spring of 1560 and ordered him to leave on Hajj to Mecca.[46] Bairam Khan left for Mecca but on his way was goaded by his opponents to rebel.[42] He was defeated by the Mughal army in Punjab and forced to submit. Akbar forgave him, however, and gave him the option of either continuing in his court or resuming his pilgrimage; Bairam chose the latter.[47] Bairam Khan was later assassinated on his way to Mecca, allegedly by an Afghan with a personal vendetta.[45]

In 1560, Akbar resumed military operations.[45] A Mughal army under the command of his foster brother, Adham Khan, and a Mughal commander, Pir Muhammad Khan, began the Mughal conquest of Malwa. The Afghan ruler, Baz Bahadur, was defeated at the Battle of Sarangpur and fled to Khandesh for refuge leaving behind his harem, treasure, and war elephants.[45] Despite initial success, the campaign proved a disaster from Akbar's point of view. His foster brother retained all the spoils and followed through with the Central Asian practice of slaughtering the surrendered garrison, their wives and children, and many Muslim theologians and Sayyids, who were the descendants of Muhammad.[45] Akbar personally rode to Malwa to confront Adham Khan and relieve him of command. Pir Muhammad Khan was then sent in pursuit of Baz Bahadur but was beaten back by the alliance of the rulers of Khandesh and Berar.[45] Baz Bahadur temporarily regained control of Malwa until, in the next year, Akbar sent another Mughal army to invade and annex the kingdom.[45] Malwa became a province of the nascent imperial administration of Akbar's regime. Baz Bahadur survived as a refugee at various courts until, eight years later in 1570, he took service under Akbar.[45]

Despite the ultimate success in Malwa, the conflict exposed cracks in Akbar's relationships with his relatives and Mughal nobles. When Adham Khan confronted Akbar following another dispute in 1562, he was struck down by the emperor and thrown from a terrace into the palace courtyard at Agra. Still alive, Adham Khan was dragged up and thrown to the courtyard once again by Akbar to ensure his death. Akbar now sought to eliminate the threat of over-mighty subjects.[45] He created specialized ministerial posts relating to imperial governance; no member of the Mughal nobility was to have unquestioned pre-eminence.[45] When a powerful clan of Uzbek chiefs broke out in rebellion in 1564, Akbar decisively defeated and routed them in Malwa and then Bihar.[48] He pardoned the rebellious leaders, hoping to conciliate them, but they rebelled again, so Akbar had to quell their uprising a second time. Following a third revolt with the proclamation of Mirza Muhammad Hakim, Akbar's brother and the Mughal ruler of Kabul, as emperor, his patience was finally exhausted. Several Uzbek chieftains were subsequently slain and the rebel leaders were trampled to death under elephants.[48] Simultaneously the Mirzas, a group of Akbar's distant cousins who held important fiefs near Agra, had also risen in rebellion. They too were slain and driven out of the empire.[48] In 1566, Akbar moved to meet the forces of his brother, Muhammad Hakim, who had marched into Punjab with dreams of seizing the imperial throne. Following a brief confrontation, however, Muhammad Hakim accepted Akbar's supremacy and retreated to Kabul.[48]

In 1564, Mughal forces began the conquest of Garha, a thinly populated, hilly area in central India that was of interest to the Mughals because of its herd of wild elephants.[49] The territory was ruled over by Raja Vir Narayan, a minor, and his mother, Durgavati, a Rajput warrior queen of the Gonds.[48] Akbar did not personally lead the campaign because he was preoccupied with the Uzbek rebellion, leaving the expedition in the hands of Asaf Khan, the Mughal governor of Kara.[48][50] Durgavati committed suicide after her defeat at the Battle of Damoh, while Raja Vir Narayan was slain at the Fall of Chauragarh, the mountain fortress of the Gonds.[50] The Mughals seized immense wealth, an uncalculated amount of gold and silver, jewels, and 1000 elephants. Kamala Devi, a younger sister of Durgavati, was sent to the Mughal harem.[50] The brother of Durgavati's deceased husband was installed as the Mughal administrator of the region.[50] Like in Malwa, however, Akbar entered into a dispute with his vassals over the conquest of Gondwana.[50] Asaf Khan was accused of keeping most of the treasures and sending back only 200 elephants to Akbar. When summoned to give accounts, he fled Gondwana. He went first to the Uzbeks, then returned to Gondwana where he was pursued by Mughal forces. Finally, he submitted and Akbar restored him to his previous position.[50]

Around 1564 is also when there was an assassination attempt on Akbar documented in a painting. The attempt was made when Akbar was returning from a visit to the dargah of Hazrat Nizamuddin near Delhi, by an assassin shooting an arrow. The arrow pierced his right shoulder. The assassin was apprehended and ordered to be beheaded by the Emperor. The culprit was a slave of Mirza

Sharfuddin, a noble in Akbar's court whose rebellion had recently been curbed.[51]

*__Mughal Emperor Akbar shoots the Rajput warrior
Jaimal during the Siege of Chittorgarh in 1568__*

Having established Mughal rule over northern India, Akbar turned his attention to the conquest of Rajputana. No imperial power in India based on the Indo-Gangetic plains could be secure if a rival center of power existed on its flank in Rajputana.[50] The Mughals had already established domination over parts of northern Rajputana in Mewat, Ajmer, and Nagor.[43][48] Now, Akbar was determined to drive into the heartlands of the Rajput kings that had never previously submitted to the Muslim rulers of the Delhi Sultanate. Beginning in 1561, the Mughals actively engaged the Rajputs in warfare and diplomacy.[49] Most Rajput states accepted Akbar's suzerainty; the rulers of Mewar and Marwar, Udai Singh and Chandrasen Rathore, however, remained outside the imperial fold.[48] Rana Udai Singh was descended from the Sisodia ruler, Rana Sanga, who had fought Babur at the Battle of Khanwa in 1527.[48] As the head of the Sisodia clan, he possessed the highest ritual status of all the Rajput kings and chieftains in India.[citation needed] Unless Udai Singh was reduced to submission, the imperial authority of the Mughals would be lessened in Rajput eyes.[48] Furthermore, Akbar, at this early period, was still enthusiastically devoted to the cause of Islam and sought to impress the superiority of his faith over the most prestigious warriors in Brahminical Hinduism.[48]

In 1567, Akbar moved to reduce the Chittor Fort in Mewar. The fortress capital of Mewar was of great strategic importance as it lay on the shortest route from Agra to Gujarat and was also considered a key to holding the interior parts of Rajputana. Udai Singh retired to the hills of Mewar, leaving two Rajput warriors, Jaimal and Patta, in charge of the defense of his capital.[52] Chittorgarh fell on February 1568 after a siege of four months. Akbar had the surviving defenders and 30,000 non-combatants massacred and their heads displayed upon towers erected throughout the region, to demonstrate his authority.[53][54] The booty that fell into the hands of the Mughals was distributed throughout the empire.[55] He remained in Chittorgarh for three days, then returned to Agra, where to commemorate the victory, he set up, at the gates of his fort, statues of Jaimal and Patta mounted on elephants.[56] Udai Singh's power and influence were broken. He never again ventured out of his mountain refuge in Mewar and Akbar was content to let him be.[57]

The fall of Chittorgarh was followed up by a Mughal attack on the Ranthambore Fort in 1568. Ranthambore was held by the Hada Rajputs and is reputed to be the most powerful fortress in India.[57] However, it fell only after a couple of months.[57] Akbar was now the master of almost the whole of Rajputana. Most of the Rajput kings had submitted to the Mughals.[57] Only the clans of Mewar continued to resist.[57] Udai Singh's son and successor, Pratap Singh, was later defeated by the Mughals at the Battle of Haldighati in 1576.[57] Akbar would celebrate his conquest of Rajputana by laying the foundation of a new capital, 23 miles (37 km) W.S.W of Agra in 1569. It was called Fatehpur Sikri ("the city of victory").[58] Rana Pratap Singh, however, continuously attacked Mughals and was able to retain most of the kingdom of his ancestors in the life of Akbar.[59]

Akbar's next military objectives were the conquest of Gujarat and Bengal, which connected India with the trading centers of Asia, Africa, and Europe through the Arabian Sea and the Bay of Bengal respectively.[57] Furthermore, Gujarat had been a haven for rebellious Mughal nobles, while in Bengal, the Afghans still held considerable influence under their ruler, Sulaiman Khan Karani. Akbar first moved against Gujarat, which lay in the crook of the Mughal provinces of Rajputana and Malwa.[57] Gujarat, with its coastal regions, possessed areas of rich agricultural production in its central plain, an impressive output of textiles and other industrial goods, and the busiest seaports in India.[57][60] Akbar intended to link the maritime state with the massive resources of the Indo-Gangetic plains.[61] However, the ostensible casus belli was that the rebel Mirzas, who had previously been driven out of India, was now operating out of a base in southern Gujarat. Moreover, Akbar had received invitations from cliques in Gujarat to oust the reigning king, which served as justification for his military expedition.[57] In 1572, he moved to occupy Ahmedabad, the capital, and other northern cities and was proclaimed the lawful sovereign of Gujarat. By 1573, he had driven out the Mirzas who, after offering token resistance, fled for refuge in the Deccan. Surat, the commercial capital of the region, and other coastal cities soon capitulated to the Mughals.[57] The king, Muzaffar Shah III, was caught hiding in a cornfield; he was pensioned off by Akbar with a small allowance.[57]

Having established his authority over Gujarat, Akbar returned to Fatehpur Sikri, where he built the Buland Darwaza to commemorate his victories, but a rebellion by Afghan nobles supported by the Rajput ruler of Idar, and the renewed intrigues of the Mirzas forced his return to Gujarat.[61] Akbar crossed the Rajputana and reached Ahmedabad in eleven days – a journey that normally took six weeks. The outnumbered Mughal army then won a decisive victory on September 2, 1573. Akbar slew the rebel leaders and erected a tower out of their severed heads.[57] The conquest and subjugation of Gujarat proved highly profitable for the Mughals; the territory yielded revenue of more than five million rupees annually to Akbar's treasury, after expenses.[57]

Akbar had now defeated most of the Afghan remnants in India. The only center of Afghan power was now in Bengal, where Sulaiman Khan Karani, an Afghan chieftain whose family had served under Sher Shah Suri, was reigning in power. While Sulaiman Khan scrupulously avoided offending Akbar, his son, Daud Khan, who had succeeded him in 1572, decided otherwise.[62] Whereas Sulaiman Khan had the khutba read in Akbar's name and acknowledged Mughal supremacy, Daud Khan assumed the insignia of royalty and ordered the khutba to be proclaimed in his name in defiance of Akbar. Munim Khan, the Mughal governor of Bihar, was ordered to chastise Daud Khan, but later, Akbar himself set out to Bengal.[62] This was an opportunity to bring the trade in the east under Mughal control.[63] In 1574, the Mughals seized Patna from Daud Khan, who fled to Bengal.[62] Akbar returned to Fatehpur Sikri and left his generals to finish the campaign. The Mughal army was subsequently victorious at the Battle of Tukaroi in 1575, which led to the annexation of Bengal and parts of Bihar that had been under the dominion of Daud Khan. Only Orissa was left in the hands of the Karani dynasty as a fief of the Mughal Empire. A year later, however, Daud Khan rebelled and attempted to regain Bengal. He was defeated by the Mughal general, Khan Jahan Quli, and had to flee into exile. Daud Khan was later captured and executed by Mughal forces. His severed head was sent to Akbar, while his limbs were gibbeted at Tanah, the Mughal capital in Bengal.[62]

Following his conquests of Gujarat and Bengal, Akbar was preoccupied with domestic concerns. He did not leave Fatehpur Sikri on a military campaign until 1581 when Punjab was again invaded by his brother, Mirza Muhammad Hakim. Akbar expelled his brother to Kabul and this time pressed on, determined to end the threat from Muhammad Hakim once and for all. In contrast to the problem that his predecessors once had in getting Mughal nobles to stay in India, the problem now was to get them to leave India. They were, according to Abul Fazl "afraid of the cold of Afghanistan." The Hindu officers, in turn, were additionally inhibited by the traditional taboo against crossing the Indus. Akbar, however, spurred them on. The soldiers were provided with pay eight months in advance. In August 1581, Akbar seized Kabul and took up residence at Babur's old citadel. He stayed there for three weeks, in the absence of his brother, who had fled into the mountains. Akbar left Kabul in the hands of his sister, Bakht-un-Nissa Begum, and returned to India. He pardoned his brother, who took up the de facto charge of the Mughal administration in Kabul; Bakht-un-Nissa continued to be the official governor. A few years later, in 1585, Muhammad Hakim died and Kabul passed into the hands of Akbar once again. It was officially incorporated as a province of the Mughal Empire.[62]

The Kabul expedition was the beginning of a long period of activity over the northern frontiers of the empire.[64] For thirteen years, beginning in 1585, Akbar remained in the north, shifting his capital to Lahore in Punjab while dealing with challenges from beyond the Khyber Pass.[64] The gravest threat came from the Uzbeks, the tribe that had driven his grandfather, Babur, out of Central Asia.[62] They had been organized under Abdullah Khan Shaybanid, a capable military chieftain who had seized Badakhshan and Balkh from Akbar's distant Timurid relatives, and whose Uzbek troops now posed a serious challenge to the northwestern frontiers of the Mughal Empire.[62][65] The Afghan tribes on the border were also restless, partly on account of the hostility of the Yusufzai of Bajaur and Swat, and partly owing to the activity of a new religious leader, Bayazid, the founder of the Roshaniyya sect.[64] The Uzbeks were also known to be subsidizing Afghans.[66]

In 1586, Akbar negotiated a pact with Abdullah Khan in which the Mughals agreed to remain neutral during the

Uzbek invasion of Safavid held Khorasan.[66] In return, Abdullah Khan agreed to refrain from supporting, subsidizing or offering refuge to the Afghan tribes hostile to the Mughals. Thus freed, Akbar began a series of campaigns to pacify the Yusufzais and other rebels.[66] Akbar ordered Zain Khan to lead an expedition against the Afghan tribes. Raja Birbal, a renowned minister in Akbar's court, was also given military command. The expedition turned out to be a disaster, and on its retreat from the mountains, Birbal and his entourage were ambushed and killed by the Afghans at the Malandarai Pass in February 1586.[66] Akbar immediately fielded new armies to reinvade the Yusufzai lands under the command of Raja Todar Mal. Over the next six years, the Mughals contained the Yusufzai in the mountain valleys and forced the submission of many chiefs in Swat and Bajaur.[66] Dozens of forts were built and occupied to secure the region. Akbar's response demonstrated his ability to clamp firm military control over the Afghan tribes.[66]

Despite his pact with the Uzbeks, Akbar nurtured a secret hope of reconquering Central Asia from today's Afghanistan.[67] However, Badakshan and Balkh remained firmly part of the Uzbek dominions. There was only a transient occupation of the two provinces by the Mughals under his grandson, Shah Jahan, in the mid-17th century.[65] Nevertheless, Akbar's stay on the northern frontiers was highly fruitful. The last of the rebellious Afghan tribes were subdued by 1600.[65] The Roshaniyya movement was firmly suppressed. The Afridi and Orakzai tribes, which had risen under the Roshaniyyas, had been subjugated.[65] The leaders of the movement were captured and driven into exile.[65] Jalaluddin, the son of the Roshaniyya movement's founder, Bayazid, was killed in 1601 in a fight with Mughal troops near Ghazni.[65] Mughal rule over today's Afghanistan was finally secure, particularly after the passing of the Uzbek threat with the death of Abdullah Khan in 1598.[66]

While in Lahore dealing with the Uzbeks, Akbar had sought to subjugate the Indus valley to secure the frontier provinces.[66] He sent an army to conquer Kashmir in the upper Indus basin when, in 1585, Ali Shah, the reigning king of the Shia Chak dynasty, refused to send his son as a hostage to the Mughal court. Ali Shah surrendered immediately to the Mughals, but another of his sons, Yaqub, crowned himself as king and led a stubborn resistance to the Mughal armies. Finally, in June 1589, Akbar himself traveled from Lahore to Srinagar to receive the surrender of Yaqub and his rebel forces.[66] Baltistan and Ladakh, which were Tibetan provinces adjacent to Kashmir, pledged their allegiance to Akbar.[68] The Mughals also moved to conquer Sindh in the lower Indus valley. Since 1574, the northern fortress of Bhakkar had remained under imperial control. Now, in 1586, the Mughal governor of Multan tried and failed to secure the capitulation of Mirza Jani Beg, the independent ruler of Thatta in southern Sindh.[66] Akbar responded by sending a Mughal army to besiege Sehwan, the river capital of the region. Jani Beg mustered a large army to meet the Mughals.[66] The outnumbered Mughal forces defeated the Sindhi forces at the Battle of Sehwan. After suffering further defeats, Jani Beg surrendered to the Mughals in 1591, and in 1593, paid homage to Akbar in Lahore.[68]

As early as 1586, about half a dozen Baluchi chiefs, under nominal Pani Afghan rule, had been persuaded to subordinate themselves to Akbar. In preparations to take Kandahar from the Safavids, Akbar ordered the Mughal forces to conquer the rest of the Afghan-held parts of Baluchistan in 1595.[68][69] The Mughal general, Mir Masum, led an attack on the stronghold of Sibi, northeast of Quetta, and defeated a coalition of local chieftains in battle.[69] They were made to acknowledge Mughal supremacy and attend Akbar's court. As a result, the modern-day Pakistani and Afghan parts of Baluchistan, including the Makran coast, became a part of the Mughal Empire.[69]

Kandahar was the name given by Arab historians to the ancient Indian kingdom of Gandhara.[70] It was intimately connected with the Mughals since the time of their ancestor, Timur, the warlord who had conquered much of Western, Central, and parts of South Asia in the 14th century. However, the Safavids considered it as an appanage of the Persian-ruled territory of Khorasan and declared its association with the Mughal emperors to be a usurpation. In 1558, while Akbar was consolidating his rule over northern India, the Safavid emperor, Tahmasp I, seized Kandahar and expelled its Mughal governor. For the next thirty years, it remained under Persian rule.[68] The recovery of Kandahar had not been a priority for Akbar, but after his prolonged military activity in the northern frontiers, a move to restore Mughal rule over the region became desirable.[68] The conquests of Sindh, Kashmir, and parts of Baluchistan, and the ongoing consolidation of Mughal power over today's Afghanistan had added to Akbar's confidence.[68] Furthermore, Kandahar was at this time under threat from the Uzbeks, but the Emperor of Persia, himself beleaguered by the Ottoman Turks, was unable to send any reinforcements. Circumstances favored the Mughals.[68]

In 1593, Akbar received the exiled Safavid prince, Rostam Mirza, after he had quarreled with his family.[71] Rostam Mirza pledged allegiance to the Mughals; he was granted a rank (mansab) of the commander of 5000 men and received Multan as a jagir.[71] Beleaguered by constant Uzbek raids, and seeing the reception of Rostom Mirza at the Mughal court, the Safavid prince and governor of Kandahar, Mozaffar Hosayn, also agreed to defect to the Mughals. Mozaffar Hosayn, who was in any case in an adversary relationship with his overlord, Shah Abbas, was granted a rank of 5000 men, and his daughter Kandahari Begum was married to Akbar's grandson, the Mughal prince, Khurram.[68][71] Kandahar was finally secured in 1595 with the arrival of a garrison headed by the Mughal general, Shah Baig Khan.[71] The reconquest of Kandahar did not overtly disturb the Mughal-Persian relationship.[68] Akbar and the Persian Shah continued to exchange ambassadors and presents. However, the power equation between the two had now changed in favor of the Mughals.[68]

In 1593, Akbar began military operations against the Deccan Sultans who had not submitted to his authority. He besieged Ahmednagar Fort in 1595, forcing Chand Bibi to cede Berar.[74] A subsequent revolt forced Akbar to take the fort in August 1600. Akbar occupied Burhanpur and besieged Asirgarh Fort in 1599, and took it on 17 January 1601, when Miran Bahadur Shah refused to submit Khandesh. Akbar then established the Subahs of Ahmadnagar, Berar, and Khandesh under Prince Daniyal. "By the time of his death in 1605, Akbar controlled a broad sweep of territory from the Bay of Bengal to Qandahar and Badakshan. He touched the western sea in Sind and at Surat and was well astride central India."[75]

CHAPTER FOUR

ADMINISTRATION

Akbar's system of the central government was based on the system that had evolved since the Delhi Sultanate, but the functions of various departments were carefully reorganized by laying down detailed regulations for their functioning

- The revenue department was headed by a wazir, responsible for all finances and management of jagir and in lands.
- The head of the military was called the Mir Bakshi, appointed from among the leading nobles of the court. The mir Bakshi was in charge of intelligence gathering, and also made recommendations to the emperor for military appointments and promotions.
- The mir saman was in charge of the imperial household, including the harems, and supervised the functioning of the court and royal bodyguard.
- The judiciary was a separate organization headed by a chief qazi, who was also responsible for religious beliefs and practices.

Akbar set about reforming the administration of his empire's land revenue by adopting a system that had been used by Sher Shah Suri. A cultivated area where crops grew well was measured and taxed through fixed rates based on the area's crop and productivity. However, this placed a hardship on the peasantry because tax rates were fixed based on prices prevailing in the imperial court, which were often higher than those in the countryside.[76] Akbar changed to a decentralized system of the annual assessment, but this resulted in corruption among local officials and was abandoned in 1580, to be replaced by a system called the dah salah.[77] Under the new system, revenue was calculated as one-third of the average produce of the previous ten years, to be paid to the state in cash. This system was later refined, taking into account local prices, and grouping areas with similar productivity into assessment circles. Remission was given to peasants when the harvest failed during times of flood or drought.[77] Akbar's dahsala system (also known as zabti) is credited to Raja Todar Mal, who also served as a revenue officer under Sher Shah Suri,[78] and the structure of the revenue administration was set out by the latter in a detailed memorandum submitted to the emperor in 1582–83.[79]

Other local methods of assessment continued in some areas. Land which was fallow or uncultivated was charged at concessional rates.[80] Akbar also actively encouraged the improvement and extension of agriculture. The village continued to remain the primary unit of revenue assessment.[81] Zamindars of every area were required to provide loans and agricultural implements in times of need, to encourage farmers to plow as much land as possible and sow seeds of superior quality. In turn, the zamindars were given a hereditary right to collect a share of the produce.

Peasants had a hereditary right to cultivate the land as long as they paid the land revenue.[80] While the revenue assessment system showed concern for the small peasantry, it also maintained a level of distrust towards the revenue officials. Revenue officials were guaranteed only three-quarters of their salary, with the remaining quarter dependent on their full realization of the revenue assessed.[82]

Akbar organized his army as well as the nobility using a system called the mansabdari. Under this system, each officer in the army was assigned a rank (a man Sardar), and assigned several cavalries that he had to supply to the imperial army.[78] The mansabdars were divided into 33 classes. The top three commanding ranks, ranging from 7,000 to 10,000 troops, were normally reserved for princes. Other ranks between 10 and 5,000 were assigned to other members of the nobility. The empire's permanent standing army was quite small and the imperial forces mostly consisted of contingents maintained by the mansabdars.[83] Persons were normally appointed to a low mansab and then promoted, based on their merit as well as the favor of the emperor.[84] Each man Sardar was required to maintain a certain number of cavalrymen and twice that number of horses. The number of horses was greater because they had to be rested and rapidly replaced in times of war. Akbar employed strict measures to ensure that the quality of the armed forces was maintained at a high level; horses were regularly inspected and only Arabian horses were normally employed.[85] The mansabdars were remunerated well for their services and constituted the highest paid military service in the world at the time.[84]

Akbar was a follower of Salim Chishti, a holy man who lived in the region of Sikri near Agra. Believing the area to be a lucky one for himself, he had a mosque constructed there for the use of the priest. Subsequently, he celebrated the victories over Chittor and Ranthambore by laying the foundation of new walled capital, 23 miles (37 km) west of Agra in 1569, which was named Fatehpur ("town of victory") after the conquest of Gujarat in 1573 and subsequently came to be known as Fatehpur Sikri to distinguish it from other similarly named towns.[52] Palaces for each of Akbar's senior queens, a huge artificial lake, and sumptuous water-filled courtyards were built there. However, the city was soon abandoned and the capital was moved to Lahore in 1585. The reason may have been that the water supply in Fatehpur Sikri was insufficient or of poor quality. Or, as some historians believe, Akbar had to attend to the northwest areas of his empire and therefore moved his capital northwest. Other sources indicate Akbar simply lost interest in the city[86] or realized it was not militarily defensible. In 1599, Akbar shifted his capital back to Agra from where he reigned until his death.

CHAPTER FIVE

ECONOMY

The reign of Akbar was characterized by commercial expansion.[87] The Mughal government encouraged traders, provided protection and security for transactions, and levied a very low custom duty to stimulate foreign trade. Furthermore, it strived to foster a climate conducive to commerce by requiring local administrators to provide restitution to traders for goods stolen while in their territory. To minimize such incidents, bands of highway police called radars were enlisted to patrol roads and ensure the safety of traders. Other active measures taken included the construction and protection of routes of commerce and communications.[88] Indeed, Akbar would make concerted efforts to improve roads to facilitate the use of wheeled vehicles through the Khyber Pass, the most popular route frequented by traders and travelers journeying from Kabul into Mughal India.[88] He also strategically occupied the northwestern cities of Multan and Lahore in Punjab and constructed great forts, such as the one at Attock near the crossing of the Grand Trunk Road and the Indus river, as well as a network of smaller forts called thanas throughout the frontier to secure the overland trade with Persia and Central Asia.[88]

Akbar was a great innovator as far as coinage is concerned. The coins of Akbar set a new chapter in India's numismatic history.[89] The coins of Akbar's grandfather, Babur, and father, Humayun, are basic and devoid of any innovation as the former was busy establishing the foundations of the Mughal rule in India while the latter was ousted by the Afghan, Sher Shah Suri, and returned to the throne only to die a year later. While the reign of both Babur and Humayun represented turmoil, Akbar's relatively long reign of 50 years allowed him to experiment with coinage.

Akbar introduced coins with decorative floral motifs, dotted borders, quatrefoil, and other types. His coins were both round and square with a unique 'mihrab' (lozenge) shape coin highlighting numismatic calligraphy at its best.[90] Akbar's portrait type gold coin (Mohur) is generally attributed to his son, Prince Salim (later Emperor Jahangir), who had rebelled and then sought reconciliation thereafter by minting and presenting his father with gold Mohur bearing Akbar's portrait. The tolerant view of Akbar is represented by the 'Ram-Sita' silver coin type while during the latter part of Akbar's reign, we see coins portraying the concept of Akbar's newly promoted religion 'Din-e-ilahi' with the Ilahi type and Jalla Jalal-Hu type coins.

The coins,[citation needed] left, represent examples of these innovative concepts introduced by Akbar that set the precedent for Mughal coins which were refined and perfected by his son, Jahangir, and later by his grandson, Shah Jahan.

CHAPTER SIX

DIPLOMACY

The practice of arranging marriages between Hindu princesses and Muslim kings was known much before Akbar's time, but in most cases, these marriages did not lead to any stable relations between the families involved, and the women were lost to their families and did not return after marriage.[91][92][93]

However, Akbar's policy of matrimonial alliances marked a departure in India from previous practice in that the marriage itself marked the beginning of a new order of relations, wherein the Hindu Rajputs who married their daughters or sisters to him would be treated on par with his Muslim fathers-in-law and brothers-in-law in all respects except being able to dine and pray with him or take Muslim wives. These Rajputs were made members of his court and their daughters' or sisters' marriage to a Muslim ceased to be a sign of degradation, except for certain proud elements who still considered it a sign of humiliation.[93]

The Kacchwaha Rajput, Raja Bharmal, of the small kingdom of Amer, who had come to Akbar's court shortly after the latter's accession, allied by giving his daughter Harka Bai, mother of Akbar's successor, in marriage to the emperor. Bharmal was made a noble of high rank in the imperial court, and subsequently, his son Bhagwant Das and grandson Man Singh also rose to high ranks in the nobility.[92]

Other Rajput kingdoms also established matrimonial alliances with Akbar, but matrimony was not insisted on as a precondition for forming alliances. Two major Rajput clans remained aloof – the Sisodiyas of Mewar and Hadas of Ranthambore. At another turning point of Akbar's reign, Raja Man Singh I of Amber went with Akbar to meet the Hada leader, Surjan Hada, to effect an alliance. Surjan accepted an alliance on the condition that Akbar did not marry any of his daughters. Consequently, no matrimonial alliance was entered into, yet Surjan was made a noble and placed in charge of Garh-Katanga.[92]

The political effect of these alliances was significant. While some Rajput women who entered Akbar's harem converted to Islam, they were generally provided full religious freedom, and their relatives, who continued to remain Hindu, formed a significant part of the nobility and served to articulate the opinions of the majority of the common populace in the imperial court.[92] The interaction between Hindu and Muslim nobles in the imperial court resulted in an exchange of thoughts and blending of the two cultures. Further, newer generations of the Mughal line represented a merger of Mughal and Rajput blood, thereby strengthening ties between the two. As a result, the Rajputs became the strongest allies of the Mughals, and Rajput soldiers and generals fought for the Mughal army under Akbar, leading it in several campaigns including the conquest of Gujarat in 1572.[94] Akbar's policy of religious tolerance ensured that employment in the imperial administration was open to all on merit irrespective of creed, and this led to an increase in the strength of the administrative services of the empire.[95]

Another legend is that Akbar's daughter Meherunnissa was enamored by Tansen and had a role in his coming to Akbar's court.[96] Tansen converted to Islam from Hinduism, apparently on the eve of his marriage with Akbar's daughter.[97][98]

At the time of Akbar's ascension in 1556, the Portuguese had established several fortresses and factories on the western coast of the subcontinent, and largely controlled navigation and sea trade in that region. As a consequence of this colonialism, all other trading entities were subject to the terms and conditions of the Portuguese, and this was resented by the rulers and traders of the time including Bahadur Shah of Gujarat.[99]

In the year 1572, the Mughal Empire annexed Gujarat and acquired its first access to the sea after local officials informed Akbar that the Portuguese had begun to exert control in the Indian Ocean. Hence Akbar was conscious of the threat posed by the presence of the Portuguese and remained content with obtaining a cart (permit) from them for sailing in the Persian Gulf region.[101] At the initial meeting of the Mughals and the Portuguese during the Siege of Surat in 1572, the Portuguese, recognizing the superior strength of the Mughal army, chose to adopt diplomacy instead of war. The Portuguese Governor, upon the request of Akbar, sent him an ambassador to establish friendly relations.[102] Akbar's efforts to purchase and secure from the Portuguese some of their compact artillery pieces were unsuccessful and thus Akbar could not establish the Mughal navy along the Gujarat coast.[103]

Akbar accepted the offer of diplomacy, but the Portuguese continually asserted their authority and power in the Indian Ocean; Akbar was highly concerned when he had to request a permit from the Portuguese before any ships from the Mughal Empire were to depart for the Hajj pilgrimage to Mecca and Medina.[104] In 1573, he issued a firman directing Mughal administrative officials in Gujarat not to provoke the Portuguese in the territory they held in Daman. The Portuguese, in turn, issued passes for the members of Akbar's family to go on Hajj to Mecca. The Portuguese made mention of the extraordinary status of the vessel and the special status to be accorded to its occupants.[105]

In September 1579 Jesuits from Goa were invited to visit the court of Akbar.[106] The emperor had his scribes translate the New Testament and granted the Jesuits freedom to preach the Gospel.[107] One of his sons, Sultan Murad Mirza, was entrusted to Antoni de Montserrat for his education.[108][109] While debating at court, the Jesuits did not confine themselves to the exposition of their own beliefs but also reviled Islam and Muhammad. Their comments enraged the Imams and Ulama, who objected to the remarks, but Akbar ordered their comments to be recorded and observed the Jesuits and their behavior. This event was followed by a rebellion of Muslim clerics in 1581 led by Mullah Muhammad Yazdi and Muiz-ul-Mulk, the chief Qadi of Bengal; the rebels wanted to overthrow Akbar and insert his brother Mirza Muhammad Hakim ruler of Kabul on the Mughal throne. Akbar successfully defeated the rebels, but he had grown more cautious about his guests and his proclamations, which he later checked with his advisers carefully.[110]

"An Emperor shall be ever Intent on Conquest, Otherwise, His enemies shall rise in arms against him.

Jalal-ud-Din Muhammad Akbar ”

In 1555, while Akbar was still a child, the Ottoman Admiral Seydi Ali Reis visited the Mughal Emperor Humayun. In 1569, during the early years of Akbar's rule, another Ottoman Admiral Kurtoğlu Hızır Reis arrived on the shores of the Mughal Empire. These Ottoman admirals sought to end the growing threats of the Portuguese Empire during their Indian Ocean campaigns. During his reign, Akbar himself is known to have sent six documents addressing the Ottoman Sultan Suleiman the Magnificent.[111][112]

In 1576 Akbar sent a very large contingent of pilgrims led by Khwaja Sultan Naqshbandi, Yahya Saleh, with 600,000 gold and silver coins and 12,000 Kaftans of honor, and large consignments of rice.[113][page needed] In October 1576 Akbar sent a delegation including members of his family, including his aunt Gulbadan Begum and his consort Salima, on Hajj by two ships from Surat including an Ottoman vessel, which reached the port of Jeddah in 1577 and then proceeded towards Mecca and Medina.[114] Four more caravans were sent from 1577 to 1580, with exquisite gifts for the authorities of Mecca and Medina.[115][116]

The imperial Mughal entourage stayed in Mecca and Medina for nearly four years and attended the Hajj four times.[117] During this period Akbar financed the pilgrimages of many poor Muslims from the Mughal Empire and also funded the foundations of the Qadiriyya Sufi Order's dervish lodge in the Hijaz.[118] The Mughals eventually set out for Surat, and their return was assisted by the Ottoman Pasha in Jeddah.[119] Because Akbar attempted to build a Mughal presence in Mecca and Medina, the local Sharifs began to have more confidence in the financial support provided by Mughal Empire, lessening their dependency upon the Ottoman bounty.[118] Mughal-Ottoman trade also flourished during this period merchants loyal to Akbar are known to have reached Aleppo after journeying upriver through the port of Basra.[120]

According to some accounts, Akbar expressed a desire to ally with the Portuguese, mainly to advance his interests, but whenever the Portuguese attempted to invade the Ottomans, Akbar proved abortive.[121][122] In 1587 a Portuguese fleet sent to attack Yemen was ferociously routed and defeated by the Ottoman Navy; thereafter the Mughal-Portuguese alliance immediately collapsed, mainly because of the continuing pressure by the Mughal Empire's prestigious vassals at Janjira.[123]

The Safavids and the Mughals had a long history of diplomatic relations, with the Safavid ruler Tahmasp I having provided refuge to Humayun when he had to flee the Indian subcontinent following his defeat by Sher Shah Suri. However, the Safavids differed from the Sunni Mughals and Ottomans in following the Shiite sect of Islam.[124] One of the longest-standing disputes between the Safavids and the Mughals pertained to the control of the city of Qandahar in the Hindukush region, forming the border between the two empires.[125] The Hindukush region was militarily very significant owing to its geography, and this was well-recognized by strategists of the times.[126] Consequently, the city, which was being administered by Bairam Khan at the time of Akbar's accession, was invaded and captured by the Persian ruler Husain Mirza, a cousin of Tahmasp I, in 1558.[125] After this, Bairam Khan sent an envoy to the court of Tahmasp I to maintain peaceful relations with the Safavids. This gesture was reciprocated and a cordial relationship continued to prevail between the two empires during the first two decades of Akbar's reign.[127] However, the death of Tahmasp I in 1576 resulted in civil war and instability in the Safavid empire, and diplomatic relations between the two empires ceased for more than a decade. They were restored only in 1587 following the accession of Shah Abbas to the Safavid throne.[128] Shortly afterward, Akbar's army completed its annexation of Kabul, and to further secure the north-western boundaries of his empire, it proceeded to Qandahar. The city capitulated without resistance on 18 April 1595, and the ruler Muzaffar Hussain moved into Akbar's court.[129] Qandahar continued to remain in Mughal possession, and the Hindukush the empire's western frontier, for several decades until Shah Jahan's expedition into Badakhshan in 1646.[130] Diplomatic relations continued to be maintained between the Safavid and Mughal courts until the end of Akbar's reign.[131]

Vincent Arthur Smith observes that the merchant Mildenhall was employed in 1600 while the establishment of the company was under adjustment to bear a letter from Queen Elizabeth to Akbar requesting liberty to trade in his dominions on terms as good as those enjoyed by the Portuguese.[132]Akbar was also visited by the French explorer Pierre Malherbe.[133]

CHAPTER SEVEN

RELIGIOUS POLICY

Akbar, as well as his mother and other members of his family, are believed to have been Sunni Hanafi Muslims.[134] His early days were spent in the backdrop of an atmosphere in which liberal sentiments were encouraged and religious narrow-mindedness was frowned upon.[135] From the 15th century, several rulers in various parts of the country adopted a more liberal policy of religious tolerance, attempting to foster communal harmony between Hindus and Muslims.[136] These sentiments were earlier encouraged by the teachings of popular saints like Guru Nanak, Kabir, and Chaitanya,[135] the verses of the Persian poet Hafez which advocated human sympathy and a liberal outlook,[137] as well as the Timurid ethos of religious tolerance in the empire, persisted in the polity right from the times of Timur to Humayun and influenced Akbar's policy of tolerance in matters of religion.[138] Further, his childhood tutors, who included two Irani Shias, were largely above sectarian prejudices and made a significant contribution to Akbar's later inclination towards religious tolerance.[138]

Akbar sponsored religious debates between different Muslim groups (Sunni, Shia, Ismaili, and Sufis), Parsis, Hindus (Shaivite and Vaishnava), Sikhs, Jains, Jews, Jesuits, and Materialists, but was partial to Sufism, he proclaimed that 'the wisdom of Vedanta is the wisdom of Sufism'.[139]

When he was at Fatehpur Sikri, he held discussions as he loved to know about others' religious beliefs. On one such day, he got to know that the religious people of other religions were often intolerant of others' religious beliefs. This led him to form the idea of the new religion, Sulh-e-Kul meaning universal peace. His idea of this religion did not discriminate against other religions and focused on the ideas of peace, unity, and tolerance.

During the early part of his reign, Akbar adopted an attitude of suppression towards Muslim sects that were condemned by the orthodoxy as heretical.[140] In 1567, on the advice of Shaikh Abdu'n Nabi, he ordered the exhumation of Mir Murtaza Sharifi Shirazi – a Shia buried in Delhi – because of the grave's proximity to that of Amir Khusrau, arguing that a "heretic" could not be buried so close to the grave of a Sunni saint, reflecting a restrictive attitude towards the Shia, which continued to persist until the early 1570s.[141] He suppressed Mahdavism in 1573 during his campaign in Gujarat, in the course of which the Mahdavi leader Bandagi Miyan Sheik Mustafa was arrested and brought in chains to the court for debate and released after eighteen months.[141] However, as Akbar increasingly came under the influence of pantheistic Sufi mysticism from the early 1570s, it caused a great shift in his outlook and culminated in his shift from orthodox Islam as traditionally professed, in favor of a new concept of Islam transcending the limits of religion.[141] Consequently, during the latter half of his reign, he adopted a policy of tolerance towards the Shias and declared a prohibition on the Shia-Sunni conflict, and the empire remained neutral in matters of internal sectarian conflict.[142] In the year 1578, the Mughal Emperor Akbar famously referred to himself as:

Emperor of Islam, Emir of the Faithful, Shadow of God on earth, Abul Fath Jalal-ud-din Muhammad Akbar Badshah Ghazi (whose empire Allah perpetuates), is the justest, most wise, and a most God-fearing ruler.

In 1580, a rebellion broke out in the eastern part of Akbar's empire, and several fatwas, declaring Akbar to be a heretic, were issued by Qazis. Akbar suppressed the rebellion and handed out severe punishments to the Qazis. To further strengthen his position in dealing with the Qazis, Akbar issued a Mazhar, or declaration, that was signed by all major ulemas in 1579.[143][144] The mahzor asserted that Akbar was the Khalifa of the age, a higher rank than that of a Mujtahid: in case of a difference of opinion among the Mujtahids, Akbar could select any one opinion and could also issue decrees that did not go against the mass.[145] Given the prevailing Islamic sectarian conflicts in various parts of the country at that time, it is believed that the Mazhar helped stabilize the religious situation in the empire.[143] It made Akbar very powerful because of the complete supremacy accorded to the Khalifa by Islam and also helped him eliminate the religious and political influence of the Ottoman Khalifa over his subjects, thus ensuring their complete loyalty to him.[146]

Throughout his reign, Akbar was a patron of influential Muslim scholars such as Mir Ahmed Nasrallah Thattvi and Tahir Muhammad That.[citation needed]

Whenever Akbar would attend congregations at a mosque the following proclamation was made:[147]

The Lord to me the Kingdom gave, He made me wise, strong and brave, He guides me through right and truth, Filling my mind with the love of truth, No praise of man could sum his state, Allah Hu Akbar, God is Great.

Akbar was deeply interested in religious and philosophical matters. An orthodox Muslim at the outset, he later came to be influenced by Sufi mysticism that was being preached in the country at that time, and moved away from orthodoxy, appointing to his court several talented people with liberal ideas, including Abul Fazl, Faizi, and Birbal. In 1575, he built a hall called the Ibadat Khana ("House of Worship") at Fatehpur Sikri, to which he invited theologians, mystics, and selected courtiers renowned for their intellectual achievements and discussed matters of spirituality with them.[135] These discussions, initially restricted to Muslims, were acrimonious and resulted in the participants shouting at and abusing each other. Upset by this, Akbar opened the Ibadat Khana to people of all religions as well as atheists, resulting in the scope of the discussions broadening and extending even into areas such as the validity of the Quran and the nature of God. This shocked the orthodox theologians, who sought to discredit Akbar by circulating rumors of his desire to forsake Islam.[143]

Akbar's effort to evolve a meeting point among the representatives of various religions was not very successful, as each of them attempted to assert the superiority of their respective religions by denouncing other religions. Meanwhile, the debates at the Ibadat Khana grew more acrimonious and, contrary to their purpose of leading to a better understanding among religions, instead led to greater bitterness among them, resulting in the discontinuance of the debates by Akbar in 1582.[148]

However, his interaction with various religious theologians had convinced him that despite their differences, all religions had several good practices, which he sought to combine into a new religious movement known as Din-i-Ilahi.[149][150]

Some modern scholars claim that Akbar did not initiate a new religion but instead introduced what Dr. Oscar R. Gómez calls the transtheistic outlook from tantric Tibetan Buddhism,[151] and that he did not use the word Din-i-Ilahi.[152] According to the contemporary events in the Mughal court Akbar was indeed angered by the acts of embezzlement of wealth by many high-level Muslim clerics.[153]

The purported Din-i-Ilahi was more of an ethical system and is said to have prohibited lust, sensuality, slander, and pride, considering them as sins. Piety, prudence, abstinence, and kindness are the core virtues. The soul is encouraged to purify itself through the yearning for God.[154] Celibacy was respected, chastity enforced, the slaughter of animals was forbidden and there were no sacred scriptures or a priestly hierarchy.[155] However, a leading Noble of Akbar's court, Aziz Koka, wrote a letter to him from Mecca in 1594 arguing that the discipleship promoted by Akbar amounted to nothing more than a desire on Akbar's part to portray his superiority regarding religious matters.[156] To commemorate Din-e-Ilahi, he changed the name of Prayag to Allahabad (pronounced as Allahabad) in 1583.[157][158]

It has been argued that the theory of Din-i-Ilahi being a new religion was a misconception that arose because of erroneous translations of Abul Fazl's work by later British historians.[159] However, it is also accepted that the policy of such-e-Kul, which formed the essence of Din-i-Ilahi, was adopted by Akbar not merely for religious purposes but as a part of general imperial administrative policy. This also formed the basis for Akbar's policy of religious toleration.[160] At the time of Akbar's death in 1605, there were no signs of discontent amongst his Muslim subjects, and the impression of even a theologian like Abdu'l Haq was that close ties remained.[161]

Akbar decreed that Hindus who had been forced to convert to Islam could reconvert to Hinduism without facing the death penalty.[162] In his days of tolerance, he was so well-liked by Hindus that there are numerous references to him, and his eulogies are sung in songs and religious hymns as well.[163]

Akbar practiced several Hindu customs. He celebrated Diwali, allowed Brahman priests to tie jeweled strings around his wrists by way of blessing, and, following his lead, many of the nobles took to wearing rakhi (protection charms).[164] He renounced beef and forbade the sale of all meats on certain days.[164]

Even his son Jahangir and grandson Shahjahan maintained many of Akbar's concessions, such as the ban on cow slaughter, having only vegetarian dishes on certain days of the week, and drinking only Ganges water.[165] Even as he was in the Punjab, 200 miles away from the Ganges, the water was sealed in large jars and transported to him. He referred to the Ganges water as the "water of immortality."[165]

Akbar regularly held discussions with Jain scholars and was also greatly impacted by their teachings. His first encounter with Jain rituals was when he saw a procession of a Jain Shravaka named Champa after a six-month-long fast. Impressed by her power and devotion, he invited her guru, or spiritual teacher, Acharya Hiravijaya Suri to

Fatehpur Sikri. Acharya accepted the invitation and began his march towards the Mughal capital from Gujarat.[166]

Akbar was impressed by the scholastic qualities and character of the Acharya. He held several inter-faith dialogues among philosophers of different religions. The arguments of Jains against eating meat persuaded him to become a vegetarian.[167] Akbar also issued many imperial orders that were favorable for Jain interests, such as banning animal slaughter.[168] Jain authors also wrote about their experience at the Mughal court in Sanskrit texts that are still largely unknown to Mughal historians.[169]

The Indian Supreme Court has cited examples of the co-existence of Jain and Mughal architecture, calling Akbar "the architect of modern India" and that "he had great respect" for Jainism. In 1584, 1592, and 1598, Akbar had declared "Amari Ghosana", which prohibited animal slaughter during Paryushan and Mahavira Janma Kalyanak. He removed the Jazia tax from Jain pilgrim places like Palitana.[170] Santichandra, the disciple of Suri, was sent to the Emperor, who in turn left his disciples Bhanuchandra and Siddhichandra in the court. Akbar again invited Hiravijaya Suri's successor Vijayasena Suri to his court who visited him between 1593 and 1595.

Akbar's religious tolerance was not followed by his son Jahangir, who even threatened Akbar's former friend Bhanuchandra.[171]

CHAPTER EIGHT

HISTORICAL ACCOUNTS

Akbar's reign was chronicled extensively by his court historian Abul Fazl in the books Akbarnama and Ain-i-Akbari. Other contemporary sources of Akbar's reign include the works of Badayuni, Shaikhzada Rashidi, and Shaikh Ahmed Sirhindi.

Akbar was a warrior, emperor, general, animal trainer (reputedly keeping thousands of hunting cheetahs during his reign and training many himself), and theologian.[172] Believed to be dyslexic, he was read to every day and had a remarkable memory.[173]

Akbar was said to have been a wise emperor and a sound judge of character. His son and heir, Jahangir, wrote effusive praise of Akbar's character in his memoirs, and dozens of anecdotes to illustrate his virtues.[174] According to Jahangir, Akbar was "of the hue of wheat; his eyes and eyebrows were black and his complexion rather dark than fair". Antoni de Montserrat, the Catalan Jesuit who visited his court described him as follows:

"One could easily recognize even at first glance that he is King. He has broad shoulders, somewhat bandy legs well-suited for horsemanship, and a light brown complexion. He carries his head bent towards the right shoulder. His forehead is broad and open, his eyes so bright and flashing that they seem like a sea shimmering in the sunlight. His eyelashes are very long. His eyebrows are not strongly marked. His nose is straight and small though not insignificant. His nostrils are wide open as though in derision. Between the left nostril and the upper lip, there is a mole. He shaves his beard but wears a mustache. He limps in his left leg though he has never received an injury there."[175]

Akbar was not tall but powerfully built and very agile. He was also noted for various acts of courage. One such incident occurred on his way back from Malwa to Agra when Akbar was 19 years of age. Akbar rode alone in advance of his escort and was confronted by a tigress who, along with her cubs, came out from the shrubbery across his path. When the tigress charged the emperor, he was alleged to have dispatched the animal with his sword in a solitary blow. His approaching attendants found the emperor standing quietly by the side of the dead animal.[176]

Abul Fazl, and even the hostile critic Badayuni, described him as having a commanding personality. He was notable for his command in battle, and, "like Alexander of Macedon, was always ready to risk his life, regardless of political consequences". He often plunged on his horse into the flooded river during the rainy seasons and safely crossed it. He rarely indulged in cruelty and is said to have been affectionate towards his relatives. He pardoned his brother Hakim, who was a repented rebel. But on rare occasions, he dealt cruelly with offenders, such as his maternal uncle Muazzam and his foster-brother Adham

Khan, who was twice defenestrated for drawing Akbar's wrath.[177]

He is said to have been extremely moderate in his diet. Ain-e-Akbari mentions that during his travels and also while at home, Akbar drank water from the Ganges river, which he called 'the water of immortality. Special people were stationed at Sorun and later Haridwar to dispatch water, in sealed jars, to wherever he was stationed.[178][better source needed] According to Jahangir's memoirs, he was fond of fruits and had little liking for meat, which he stopped eating in his later years.

Akbar also once visited Vrindavan, regarded as the birthplace of Krishna, in the year 1570, and permitted four temples to be built by the Gaudiya Vaishnavas, which were Madana-Mohana, Govindaji, Gopinatha, and Jugal Kishore.

To defend his stance that speech arose from hearing, he carried out a language deprivation experiment, and had children raised in isolation, not allowed to be spoken to, and pointed out that as they grew older, they remained mute.[179]

During Akbar's reign, the ongoing process of inter-religious discourse and syncretism resulted in a series of religious attributions to him in terms of positions of assimilation, doubt, or uncertainty, which he either assisted himself or left unchallenged.[180] Such hagiographical accounts of Akbar traversed a wide range of denominational and sectarian spaces, including several accounts by Parsis, Jains, and Jesuit missionaries, apart from contemporary accounts by Brahminical and Muslim orthodoxy.[181] Existing sects and denominations, as well as various religious figures who represented popular worship, felt they had a claim to him. The diversity of these accounts is attributed to the fact that his reign resulted in the formation of a flexible centralized state accompanied by personal authority and cultural heterogeneity.[180]

The Akbarnāma (Persian: اکبر نامہ), which means Book of Akbar, is an official biographical account of Akbar, the third Mughal Emperor (r. 1542–1605), written in Persian. It includes vivid and detailed descriptions of his life and times.[182]

The work was commissioned by Akbar, and written by Abul Fazl, one of the Nine Jewels (Hindi: Navaratnas) of Akbar's royal court. It is stated that the book took seven years to be completed and the original manuscripts contained several paintings supporting the texts, and all the paintings represented the Mughal school of painting, and the work of masters of the imperial workshop, including Basawan, whose use of portraiture in its illustrations was an innovation in Indian art.[182]

CHAPTER NINE

CONSORTS

Akbar's first wife and one of the chief consorts was his cousin, Princess Ruqaiya Sultan Begum,[27][4] the only daughter of his paternal uncle, Prince Hindal Mirza,[183] and his wife Sultana Begum. In 1551, Hindal Mirza died fighting valorously in a battle against Kamran Mirza's forces. Upon hearing the news of his brother's death, Humayun was overwhelmed with grief.[23] Hindal's daughter Ruqaiya married Akbar about the time of his first appointment, at age nine, as governor of Ghazni Province.[24] Humayun conferred on the imperial couple, all the wealth, army, and adherents of Hindal and Ghazni which one of Hindal's jagir was given to his nephew, Akbar, who was appointed as its viceroy and was also given the command of his uncle's army.[25] Akbar's marriage with Ruqaiya was solemnized near Jalandhar, Punjab when both of them were 14-years-old.[26]

His second wife was the daughter of Abdullah Khan Mughal.[184] The marriage took place in 1557 during the siege of Manko. Bairam Khan did not approve of this marriage, for Abdullah's sister was married to Akbar's uncle, Prince Kamran Mirza, and so he regarded Abdullah as a partisan of Kamran. He opposed the match until Nasir-al-Mulk made him understand that opposition in such matters was unacceptable. Nasir-al-Mulk arranged an assemblage of pleasure and banquet of joy, and a royal feast was provided.[185]

His third wife and one of his three chief consorts was his cousin, Salima Sultan Begum,[184] the daughter of Nur-ud-din Muhammad Mirza, and his wife Gulrukh Begum also known as Gulrang, the daughter of Emperor Babur. She was at first betrothed to Bairam Khan by Humayun. After Bairam Khan died in 1561, Akbar married her in the same year. She was the foster mother of Akbar's second son, Murad Mirza. She held a great influence on Akbar. She was a poetess and was regarded as an exceptional woman being a skilled writer and playing an active role in the politics of the Mughal court during Akbar's and Jahangir's reigns. She died childless on 2 January 1613.[186]

His fourth wife and one of his three chief consorts was the beautiful daughter of Raja Bharmal, ruler of Amer, Harka Bai whom he married in the year 1562. She gradually became his favorite and most influential consort and subsequently is the only wife buried close to him. She was bestowed with the honorific name of 'Wali Nimat begum' (Blessings of God) shortly after her marriage. She was an extremely beautiful woman said to possess uncommon beauty. Widely known for her beauty, grace, and intellect, she was a secular, amiable, sensible, and virtuous woman who was the prime driving force for Akbar's promotion of secularism. This marriage took place when Akbar was on his way back from Ajmer after offering prayers to the tomb of Moinuddin Chishti. Bharmal had conveyed to Akbar that he was being harassed by his brother-in-law Sharif-ud-din Mirza (the Mughal hakim of Mewat). Akbar insisted that Bharmal should submit to him personally, it was also suggested that his beautiful daughter should be married to him as a sign of complete submission.[187] She became his first wife to honor the royal mansion with an heir. In the year 1564, she gave birth to twins named Mirza Hassan and Mirza Hussain. In the year 1569, she was honored with the prestigious title of Mariam-uz-Zamani after giving birth to another son named Prince Salim (the future emperor Jahangir), the heir to the throne. She was also the foster mother of Akbar's favorite son, Daniyal Mirza. She was bestowed with three more titles of 'Mallika-e-Hindustan', 'Mallika-e-Muezamma' (Exalted Empress), and 'Shahi Begum' (Imperial Begum). As stated by Abul Fazl in Akbarnama, the Empress is said to have commanded a high rank in the imperial harem. She was a smart woman who established the international trade in the Mughal Empire and was the only wife of Akbar who had been authorized for the trade. In her time she was regarded as the most adventurous and fearsome businesswoman. She died on 19 May 1623 in Agra and was buried close to her husband in Sikandra. [188]

In the year 1562, Akbar married the former wife of Abdul Wasi, the son of Shaikh Bada, lord of Agra. Akbar was enamored with her beauty and ordered Abdul Wasi to divorce her.[189] Another of his wives was Gauhar-un-Nissa Begum, the daughter of Shaikh Muhammad Bakhtiyar and the sister of Shaikh Jamal Bakhtiyar. Their dynasty was called Din Laqab and had been living for a long time in Chandler and Jalesar near Agra.[190] He married the daughter of Jagmal Rathore, son of Rao Viramde of Merta in 1562.[191]

His next marriage took place in 1564 to the daughter of Miran Mubarak Shah, the ruler of Khandesh. In 1564, he sent presents to the court with a request that his daughter is married to Akbar. Miran's request acceded and an order was issued. Imad Khan was sent with Miran's ambassadors, and when he came near the fort of Asir, which was Miran's residence. Miran welcomed Itimad with honor and despatched his daughter with Imad. A large number of nobles accompanied her. The marriage took place in September 1564 when she reached Akbar's court.[192] As a dowry, Mubarak Shah ceded Bijagarh and Handia to his imperial son-in-law.[193]

He married another Rajput princess in 1570, Raj Kanwar, daughter of Kanha, the brother of Rai Kalyan Mal, the ruler of Bikaner.[194] The marriage took place in 1570 when Akbar came to this part of the country. Kalyan made a homage to Akbar and requested that his brother's daughter be married to him. Akbar accepted his proposal, and the marriage was arranged.[195] He also married Bhanmati, daughter of Bhim Raj, another brother of Rai Kalyan Mal.[194] He also married Nathi Bai, daughter of Rawal Har Rai, the ruler of Jaisalmer in 1570.[196][197][198] Rawal had sent a request that his daughter is married to Akbar. The proposal was accepted by Akbar. Raja Bhagwan Das was despatched on this service. The marriage ceremony took place after Akbar's return from Nagor.[199] She was the mother of Princess Mahi Begum, who died on 8 April 1577.[200] In 1570, Narhardas, a grandson of Rao Viramde of Merta, married his sister, Puram Bai, to Akbar in return for Akbar's support of Keshodas's claims on Merta.[201][202]

Another of his wives was Bhakkari Begum, the daughter of Sultan Mahmud of Bhakkar.[203] On 2 July 1572, Akbar's envoy I'timad Khan reached Mahmud's court to escort his daughter to Akbar. Intimate Khan brought with him for Sultan Mahmud an elegant dress of honor, a bejeweled scimitar belt, a horse with a saddle and reins, and four elephants. Mahmud celebrated the occasion by holding extravagant feasts for fifteen days. On the day of the wedding, the festivities reached their zenith, and the ulema, saints, and nobles were adequately honored with rewards. Mahmud offered 30,000 rupees in cash and kind to I'timad Khan and farewelled his daughter with a grand dowry and an impressive entourage.[204] She came to Ajmer and waited upon Akbar. The gifts of Sultan Mahmud, carried by the delegation were presented to the ladies of the imperial harem.[205]

His ninth wife was Qasima Banu Begum,[184] the daughter of Arab Shah. The marriage took place in 1575. A great feast was given, and the high officers and other pillars of the state were present.[206] In 1577, the Rawal Askaran of Dungarpur State petitioned a request that his daughter might be married to Akbar. Akbar had regard for his loyalty and granted his request.[207] Rai Loukaran and Rajah Birbar, servants of the Rajah were sent from Dihalpur to do the honor of conveying his daughter. The two delivered the lady at Akbar's court where the marriage took place on 12 July 1577.[208]

His eleventh wife was Bibi Daulat Shad.[184] She was the mother of Princess Shakr-un-Nissa Begum, and Princess Aram Banu Begum[209] born on 22 December 1584.[210][211] His next wife was the daughter of Shams Chak, a Kashmiri. The marriage took place on 3 November 1592. Shams belonged to the great men of the country and had long cherished this wish.[212] In 1593, he married the daughter of Qazi Isa and the cousin of Najib Khan. Najib told Akbar that his uncle had made his daughter a present for him. Akbar accepted his representation and on 3 July 1593, he visited Najib Khan's house and married Qazi Isa's daughter.[213]

At some point, Akbar took into his harem Rukmavati, a daughter of Rao Maldev of Marwar by one of his mistresses. This was a dolo union as opposed to formal marriage, representing the bride's lower status in her father's household, and served as an expression of vassalage to an overlord. The dating of this event is not recorded.[214][215]

CHAPTER TEN

DEATH AND LEGACY

On 3 October 1605, Akbar fell ill from an attack of dysentery[216] from which he never recovered. He is believed to have died on 27 October 1605. He was buried at his mausoleum in Sikandra, Agra which lies a kilometer next to the tomb of Mariam-uz-Zamani, his favorite and chief consort.[217]

Akbar left a rich legacy both for the Mughal Empire as well as the Indian subcontinent in general. He firmly entrenched the authority of the Mughal Empire in India and beyond, after it had been threatened by the Afghans during his father's reign,[218] establishing its military and diplomatic superiority.[219] During his reign, the nature of the state changed to a secular and liberal one, with emphasis on cultural integration. He also introduced several far-sighted social reforms, including prohibiting sati, legalizing widow remarriage, and raising the age of marriage. Folk tales revolving around him and Birbal, one of his navratnas, are popular in India. He and his Hindu wife, Mariam-uz-Zamani, in the popular culture known as 'Jodha Bai' are widely famous as the latter is believed to have been the prime inspiration and driving force for Akbar's promotion of secularism.

Bhavishya Purana is a minor Purana that depicts the various Hindu holy days and includes a section devoted to the various dynasties that ruled India, dating its oldest portion to 500 CE and newest to the 18th century. It contains a story about Akbar in which he is compared to the other Mughal rulers. The section called "Akbar Bahshaha Varnan", written in Sanskrit describes his birth as a "reincarnation" of a sage who immolated himself on seeing the first Mughal ruler Babur, who is described as the "cruel king of Mlecchas (Muslims)". In this text it is stated that Akbar "was a miraculous child" and that he would not follow the previous "violent ways" of the Mughals.[220][221]

Citing Akbar's melding of the disparate 'fiefdoms' of India into the Mughal Empire as well as the lasting legacy of "pluralism and tolerance" that "underlies the values of the modern republic of India", Time magazine included his name in its list of top 25 world leaders.[15]

On the other hand, his legacy is explicitly negative in Pakistan for the same reasons. Historian Mubarak Ali, while studying the image of Akbar in Pakistani textbooks, observes that Akbar "is conveniently ignored and not mentioned in any school textbook from class one to matriculation", as opposed to the omnipresence of emperor Aurangzeb. He quotes historian Ishtiaq Hussain Qureshi, who said that, due to his religious tolerance, "Akbar had so weakened Islam through his policies that it could not be restored to its dominant position in the affairs." A common thread among Pakistani historians is to blame Akbar's Rajput policy. In a conclusion, after analyzing many textbooks, Mubarak Ali says that "Akbar is criticized for bringing Muslims and Hindus together as one nation and putting the separate identity of the Muslims in danger. This policy of Akbar contradicts the theory of Two-Nation and therefore makes him an unpopular figure in Pakistan."[222]

References

1. Eraly, Abraham (2004). The Mughal Throne: The Saga of India's Great Emperors. Phoenix. pp. 115, 116. ISBN 978-0-7538-1758-2.

2. ^ "Akbar (Mughal emperor)". Encyclopædia Britannica. Retrieved 18 January 2013.

3. ^ Chandra, Satish (2005). Medieval India : from Sultanat to the Mughals (Revised ed.). New Delhi: Har-Anand Publications. p. 95. ISBN 978-8124110669.

4. ^ Jump up to:a b c Jahangir, Emperor of Hindustan (1999). The Jahangirnama: Memoirs of Jahangir, Emperor of India. Translated by Thackston, Wheeler M. Oxford University Press. p. 437. ISBN 978-0-19-512718-8. Ruqayya-Sultan Begam, the daughter of Mirza Hindal and wife of His Majesty Arsh-Ashyani [Akbar], had passed away in Akbarabad. She was His Majesty's chief wife. Since she did not have children, when Shahjahan was born His Majesty Arsh-Ashyani entrusted that "unique pearl of the caliphate" to the begam's care, and she undertook to raise the prince. She departed this life at the age of eighty-four.

5. ^ Robinson, Annemarie Schimmel (2005). Waghmar, Burzine K. (ed.). The empire of the Great Mughals : history, art and culture. Translated by Attwood, Corinne (Revised ed.). Lahore: Sang-E-Meel Pub. p. 145. ISBN 9781861891853.

6. ^ Hindu Shah, Muhammad Qasim. Gulshan-I-Ibrahimi. p. 223.

7. ^ Mehta, J.L. (1981). Advance Study in the history of Medieval India. Vol. III. Sterling Publisher Private

Limited. ISBN 8120704320. Bihari Mal gave rich dowry to his daughter and sent his son Bhagwan Das with a contingent of Rajput soldiers to escort his newly married sister to Agra as per Hindu custom. Akbar was deeply impressed by the highly dignified, sincere and princely conduct of his Rajput relations. He took Man Singh, the youthful son of Bhagwant Das into the royal service. Akbar was fascinated by the charm and accomplishments of his Rajput wife; he developed real love for her and raised her to the status of chief queen. She came to exercise profound impact on socio-cultural environment of the entire royal household and changed the lifestyle of Akbar. Salim (later Jahangir), heir to the throne, was born of this wedlock on 30th August, 1569.

8. ^ Jump up to:a b Ballhatchet, Kenneth A. "Akbar". Encyclopædia Britannica. Retrieved 17 July 2017.

9. ^ Black, Antony (2011). The History of Islamic Political Thought: From the Prophet to the Present. Edinburgh University Press. p. 245. ISBN 978-0748688784.

10. ^ Eraly, Abraham (2000). Emperors of the Peacock Throne : The Saga of the Great Mughals. Penguin books. p. 189. ISBN 978-0-14-100143-2.

11. ^ "Akbar I". Encyclopaedia Iranica. 29 July 2011. Retrieved 18 January 2014.

12. ^ Jump up to:a b "Akbar I". Oxford Reference. 17 February 2012. doi:10.1093/acref/ 9780199546091.001.0001. ISBN 9780199546091.

13. ^ Fazl, Abul. The Akbarnama. Translated by Beveridge, Henry. ASIATIC SOCIETY OF BENGAL. pp. 139–140.

14. ^ Syed, Jawad (2011). "Akbar's multiculturalism: lessons for diversity management in the 21st century". Canadian Journal of Administrative Sciences. John Wiley & Sons, Ltd. 28 (4): 404. doi:10.1002/CJAS.185.

15. ^ Jump up to:a b Tharoor, Ishaan (4 February 2011). "Top 25 Political Icons:Akbar the Great". Time. Archived from the original on 7 February 2011.

16. ^ Jump up to:a b Murray, Stuart. 2009. The library: an illustrated history. Chicago, ALA Editions

17. ^ Wiegand & Davis, Jr. 1994, p. 273.

18. ^ Banjerji, S.K. (1938). Humayun Badshah. Oxford University Press.

19. ^ Smith 1917, pp. 18–19

20. ^ Smith 1917, pp. 12–19

21. ^ Fazl, Abul. Akbarnama Volume I.

22. ^ Smith 1917, p. 22

23. ^ Jump up to:a b Erskine, William (1854). A History of India Under the Two First Sovereigns of the House of Taimur, Báber and Humáyun, Volume 2. Longman, Brown, Green, and Longmans. pp. 403, 404. ISBN 978-1108046206.

24. ^ Jump up to:a b Mehta, Jaswant Lal (1984) [First published 1981]. Advanced Study in the History of Medieval India. Vol. II (2nd ed.). Sterling Publishers. p. 189. ISBN 978-81-207-1015-3. OCLC 1008395679.

25. ^ Jump up to:a b Ferishta, Mahomed Kasim (2013). History of the Rise of the Mahomedan Power in India, Till the Year AD 1612. Cambridge University Press. p. 169. ISBN 978-1-108-05555-0.

26. ^ Jump up to:a b Eraly, Abraham (2000). Emperors of the Peacock Throne : the saga of the great Mughals. Penguin books. pp. 123, 272. ISBN 978-0141001432.

27. ^ Jump up to:a b Schimmel, Annemarie (2005). Waghmar, Burzine K. (ed.). The empire of the Great Mughals : history, art and culture. Translated by Attwood, Corinne (Revised ed.). Lahore: Sang-E-Meel Pub. p. 149. ISBN 978-1861891853.

28. ^ "Akbar, the Great Mughal". Nature. 150 (3812): 600–601. 21 November 1942. Bibcode:1942Natur.150R.600.. doi:10.1038/150600b0. S2CID 4084248. Retrieved 31 January 2021.

29. ^ Jump up to:a b c "Remembering Akbar the Great: Facts about the most liberal Mughal emperor". India Today. 27 October 2016. Retrieved 31 January 2021.

30. ^ "Gurdas". Government of Punjab. Archived from the original on 27 May 2008. Retrieved 30 May 2008.

31. ^ History Archived 2 August 2005 at the Wayback Machine Gurdaspur district website.

32. ^ Smith 2002, p. 337

33. ^ Jump up to:a b Lal, Ruby (2005). Domesticity and Power in the Early Mughal World. Cambridge University Press. p. 140. ISBN 978-0-521-85022-3.

34. ^ Jump up to:a b Kulke, Hermann (2004). A history of India. Routledge. p. 205. ISBN 978-0-415-32920-0.

35. ^ Schimmel, Annemarie (2004). The Empire of the Great Mughals: History, Art, and Culture. Reaktion Books. p. 88. ISBN 978-1-86189-185-3.

36. ^ Richards, John F. (1996). The Mughal Empire. Cambridge University Press. p. 288. ISBN 978-0-521-56603-2.

37. ^ Elgood, Robert (1995). Firearms of the Islamic World. I.B. Tauris. p. 135. ISBN 978-1-85043-963-9.

38. ^ Gommans, Jos (2002). Mughal Warfare: Indian Frontiers and High Roads to Empire, 1500–1700. Routledge. p. 134. ISBN 978-0-415-23988-2.

39. ^ Jump up to:a b c d e Eraly, Abraham (2000). Emperors of the Peacock Throne: The Saga of the Great Mughals. Penguin Books India. pp. 118–124. ISBN 978-0-14-100143-2.

40. ^ Majumdar 1974, p. 104: "But the arch-enemy was

neither Sikandar, who had become a spent force after Māchīwārā and Sirhind"

41. ^ Chandra 2007, pp. 226–227

42. ^ Jump up to:a b Chandra 2007, p. 227

43. ^ Jump up to:a b c d e Richards, John F. (1996). The Mughal Empire. Cambridge University Press. pp. 9–13. ISBN 978-0-521-56603-2.

44. ^ Morgan, David O.; Reid, Anthony, eds. (2010). The New Cambridge History of Islam, Volume 3: The Eastern Islamic World, Eleventh to Eighteenth Centuries. Cambridge: Cambridge University Press. ISBN 978-0-521-85031-5.

45. ^ Jump up to:a b c d e f g h i j k Richards, John F. (1996). The Mughal Empire. Cambridge University Press. pp. 14–15. ISBN 978-0-521-56603-2.

46. ^ Smith 2002, p. 339

47. ^ Chandra 2007, p. 228

48. ^ Jump up to:a b c d e f g h i j k Eraly, Abraham (2000). Emperors of the Peacock Throne: The Saga of the Great Mughals. Penguin Books India. pp. 140–141. ISBN 978-0-14-100143-2.

49. ^ Jump up to:a b Richards, John F. (1996). The Mughal Empire. Cambridge University Press. pp. 17–21. ISBN 978-0-521-56603-2.

50. ^ Jump up to:a b c d e f g Chandra, Satish (2005). Medieval India: From Sultanat to the Mughals, Part II. Har-Anand Publications. pp. 105–106. ISBN 978-81-241-1066-9.

51. ^ Irfan, Lubna. "The Woman Whose Downfall Nearly Killed Akbar". TheWire. Retrieved 11 May 2020.

52. ^ Jump up to:a b Chandra 2007, p. 231

53. ^ Smith 2002, p. 342

54. ^ Chandra, Satish (2001). Medieval India: From Sultanat to the Mughals Part I. Har-Anand Publications. p. 107. ISBN 81-241-0522-7.

55. ^ Payne, Tod (1994). Tod's Annals of Rajasthan: The Annals of Mewar. Asian Educational Services. p. 71. ISBN 81-206-0350-8.

56. ^ Eraly, Abraham (2007). The Mughal World. Penguin Books India. p. 11. ISBN 978-0-14-100143-2.

57. ^ Jump up to:a b c d e f g h i j k l m n Eraly, Abraham (2000). Emperors of the Peacock Throne: The Saga of the Great Mughals. Penguin Books India. pp. 143–147. ISBN 978-0-14-100143-2.

58. ^ Hastings, James (2003). Encyclopedia of Religion and Ethics Part 10. Kessinger Publishing. ISBN 0-7661-3682-5.

59. ^ "Rana Pratap Singh | Indian ruler". Encyclopædia Britannica.

60. ^ Chandra 2007, p. 232

61. ^ Jump up to:a b Richards, John F. (1996). The Mughal Empire. Cambridge University Press. p. 32. ISBN 978-0-521-56603-2.

62. ^ Jump up to:a b c d e f g Eraly, Abraham (2000). Emperors of the Peacock Throne: The Saga of the Great Mughals. Penguin Books India. pp. 148–154. ISBN 978-0-14-100143-2.

63. ^ Pletcher, Kenneth (2010). Emperors of the Peacock Throne: The Saga of the Great Mughals. The Rosen Publishing Group. p. 170. ISBN 978-1-61530-201-7.

64. ^ Jump up to:a b c "The Age of Akbar". columbia.edu. Retrieved 31 May 2013.

65. ^ Jump up to:a b c d e f Dani, Ahmad Hasan Dani; Chahryar Adle; Irfan Habib (2002). History of Civilizations of Central Asia: Development in Contrast:

From the Sixteenth to the Mid-Nineteenth Century. UNESCO. pp. 276–277. ISBN 978-92-3-102719-2.

66. ^ Jump up to:a b c d e f g h i j k Richards, John F. (1996). The Mughal Empire. Cambridge University Press. pp. 49–51. ISBN 978-0-521-56603-2.

67. ^ Markovitz, Claude (2002). A History of Modern India: 1480–1950. Anthem Press. p. 93. ISBN 978-1-84331-004-4.

68. ^ Jump up to:a b c d e f g h i j Eraly, Abraham (2000). Emperors of the Peacock Throne: The Saga of the Great Mughals. Penguin Books India. pp. 156–157. ISBN 978-0-14-100143-2.

69. ^ Jump up to:a b c Mehta, J. L. (1984) [First published 1981]. Advanced Study in the History of Medieval India. Vol. II (2nd ed.). Sterling Publishers. p. 258. ISBN 978-81-207-1015-3. OCLC 1008395679.

70. ^ Houtsma, M.T. (1993). E. J. Brill's First Encyclopaedia of Islam, 1913–1936, Volume 4. Brill. p. 711. ISBN 978-90-04-09796-4.

71. ^ Jump up to:a b c d Floor, Willem; Edmund Herzig (2012). Iran and the World in the Safavid Age. I.B. Tauris. p. 136. ISBN 978-1-85043-930-1.

72. ^ Smith 1917, p. 274.

73. ^ Gibbs, J. (1865). Proceedings of the Asiatic Society of Bengal. Calcutta. pp. 4–5.

74. ^ Adibah, Sulaiman (December 2017). "Akbar (1556-1605) and India unification under the mughals". ResearchGate. 8 (12). Retrieved 31 January 2021.

75. ^ Sen, Sailendra (2013). A Textbook of Medieval Indian History. Primus Books. pp. 164, 188. ISBN 978-93-80607-34-4.

76. ^ Chandra 2007, p. 233

77. ^ Jump up to:a b Chandra 2007, p. 234

78. ^ Jump up to:a b Chandra 2007, p. 236
79. ^ Moosvi 2008, p. 160
80. ^ Jump up to:a b Chandra 2007, p. 235
81. ^ Moosvi 2008, pp. 164–165
82. ^ Moosvi 2008, p. 165
83. ^ Smith 2002, p. 359
84. ^ Jump up to:a b Chandra 2007, p. 238
85. ^ Chandra 2007, p. 237
86. ^ Petersen, A. (1996). Dictionary of Islamic Architecture. New York: Routledge.
87. ^ "Economic and Social Developments under the Mughals". columbia.edu. Retrieved 30 May 2013.
88. ^ Jump up to:a b c Levi, S. C. (2002). The Indian Diaspora in Central Asia and Its Trade: 1550–1900. Brill. p. 39. ISBN 978-90-04-12320-5.
89. ^ "Mughal Coins - Akbar". indian-coins.com. Retrieved 20 July 2020.
90. ^ "Coins of Akbar | Mintage World". 29 July 2016. Retrieved 20 July 2020.
91. ^ Eraly, Abraham (2000). Emperors of the Peacock Throne, The Saga of the Great Mughals. Penguin Books India. p. 136. ISBN 0-14-100143-7.
92. ^ Jump up to:a b c d Chandra 2007, p. 243
93. ^ Jump up to:a b Sarkar 1984, p. 37
94. ^ Sarkar 1984, pp. 38–40
95. ^ Sarkar 1984, p. 38
96. ^ Maryam Juzer Kherulla (12 October 2002). "Profile: Tansen – the mesmerizing maestro". Dawn. Archived from the original on 21 November 2007. Retrieved 2 October 2007.
97. ^ India Divided, By Rajendra Prasad, p. 63
98. ^ A History of Hindi Literature, By F. E. Keay, p. 36
99. ^ Habib 1997, p. 256

100. ^ Dodwell, Henry H., ed. (1929). The Cambridge history of the British Empire. Vol. IV. Cambridge: The University Press. p. 14. OCLC 1473561.
101. ^ Habib 1997, pp. 256–257
102. ^ Habib 1997, p. 259
103. ^ Frances Pritchett. "XVI. Mughal Administration". Columbia.edu. Retrieved 18 January 2014.
104. ^ Frances Pritchett. "XIX. A Century of Political Decline: 1707–1803". Columbia.edu. Retrieved 18 January 2014.
105. ^ Habib 1997, p. 260
106. ^ Akbar's letter of invitation in: John Correia-Afonso, Letters from the Mughal Court, Bombay, 1980.
107. ^ Gomez, Oscar R (2013). Tantrism in the Society of Jesus – from Tibet to the Vaticcan today. Editorial MenteClara. p. 58. ISBN 978-987-24510-3-5.
108. ^ du Jarric, Pierre (1926). Akbar and the Jesuits. Broadway Travellers. Translated by Payne, C. H. London: Harper & Brothers.
109. ^ Durant, Will (7 June 2011). Our Oriental Heritage: The Story of Civilization. Simon and Schuster. pp. 738–. ISBN 978-1-4516-4668-9. Retrieved 27 August 2012.
110. ^ Frances Pritchett. "XII. Religion at Akbar's Court". Columbia.edu. Retrieved 18 January 2014.
111. ^ N. R. Farooqi (1996). "Six Ottoman Documents on Mughal-Ottoman Relations During The Reign of Akbar". Journal of Islamic Studies. 7 (1): 32. doi:10.1093/jis/7.1.32. Archived from the original on 2 March 2012. Retrieved 18 January 2014.
112. ^ Sanjay Subrahmanyam (1 June 1994). "Book Reviews: Naimur Rahman Farooqi, Mughal-Ottoman Relations: A Study of the Political and Diplomatic Relations between Mughal India and the Ottoman Empire, 1556–1748,

Delhi". The Indian Economic & Social History Review. 31 (2): 249. doi:10.1177/001946469403100210. S2CID 143346476. Retrieved 18 January 2014.

113. ^ Farooqi, Naimur Rahman (1989). Mughal-Ottoman relations: a study of political & diplomatic relations between Mughal India and the Ottoman Empire, 1556–1748. Delhi: Idarah-i Adabiyat-i Delli. OCLC 20894584.

114. ^ Moosvi 2008, p. 246

115. ^ Ottoman court chroniclers (1578). Muhimme Defterleri, Vol. 32 f 292 firman 740, Shaban 986.

116. ^ Khan, Iqtidar Alam (1999). Akbar and his age. Northern Book Centre. p. 218. ISBN 978-81-7211-108-3.

117. ^ Farooqi, N. R. (21 March 2017). "An Overview of Ottoman Archival Documents and Their Relevance for Medieval Indian History". The Medieval History Journal. 20: 192–229. doi:10.1177/0971945816687687. S2CID 164261762.

118. ^ Jump up to:a b Faroqhi 2006, p. 88

119. ^ Farooqi, Naimur Rahman (1989). Mughal-Ottoman relations: a study of political & diplomatic relations between Mughal India and the Ottoman Empire, 1556–1748. Delhi: Idarah-i Adabiyat-i Delli. OCLC 20894584.

120. ^ Faroqhi 2006, p. 138

121. ^ Farooqi, Naimur Rahman (1989). Mughal-Ottoman relations: a study of political & diplomatic relations between Mughal India and the Ottoman Empire, 1556–1748. Delhi: Idarah-i Adabiyat-i Delli. OCLC 20894584.

122. ^ Majumdar 1984, p. 158

123. ^ Ottoman court chroniclers (1588). Muhimme

Defterleri, Vol. 62 f 205 firman 457, Avail Rabiulavval 996.

124. ^ Ali 2006, p. 94
125. ^ Jump up to:a b Majumdar 1984, p. 153
126. ^ Ali 2006, pp. 327–328
127. ^ Majumdar 1984, p. 154
128. ^ Majumdar 1984, pp. 154–155
129. ^ Majumdar 1984, pp. 153–154
130. ^ Ali 2006, p. 327
131. ^ Majumdar 1984, p. 155
132. ^ Smith 1917, p. 292
133. ^ Asia in the Making of Europe, Volume III: A Century of Advance. Book 1 by Donald F. Lach, Edwin J. Van Kley p. 393 [1]
134. ^ Habib 1997, p. 80
135. ^ Jump up to:a b c Chandra 2007, p. 253
136. ^ Chandra 2007, p. 252
137. ^ Hasan 2007, p. 72
138. ^ Jump up to:a b Habib 1997, p. 81
139. ^ Doniger, Wendy (March 2014). On Hinduism. Oxford. ISBN 978-0199360079. OCLC 858660095.
140. ^ Habib 1997, p. 85
141. ^ Jump up to:a b c Habib 1997, p. 86
142. ^ Ali 2006, pp. 165–166
143. ^ Jump up to:a b c Chandra 2007, p. 254
144. ^ Ali 2006, p. 159
145. ^ Hasan 2007, p. 79
146. ^ Hasan 2007, pp. 82–83
147. ^ Keene, Henry George (1879). The Turks in India. London: W. H. Allen. OCLC 613242467.
148. ^ Chandra 2007, p. 255
149. ^ Chandra 2007, p. 256
150. ^ "Din-i Ilahi – Britannica Online Encyclopedia".

Encyclopædia Britannica. Retrieved 18 July 2009.

151. ^ Gómez, Oscar R. (2013). Tantrism in the Society of Jesus – from Tibet to the Vaticcan today. Editorial MenteClara. p. 51. ISBN 978-987-24510-3-5.

152. ^ Sharma, Sri Ram (1988). The Religious Policy of the Mughal Emperors. Munshiram Manoharlal Publishers. p. 42. ISBN 81-215-0395-7.

153. ^ Smith 2002, p. 348

154. ^ Roy Choudhury, Makhan Lal (1985) [First published 1941]. The Din-i-Ilahi, or, The religion of Akbar (3rd ed.). New Delhi: Oriental Reprint. ISBN 81-215-0777-4.

155. ^ Majumdar 1984, p. 138

156. ^ Koka, Aziz (1594). King's College Collection, MS 194. This letter is preserved in Cambridge University Library. p. ff.5b–8b.

157. ^ Conder, Josiah (1828). The Modern Traveller: a popular description. R.H.Tims. p. 282.

158. ^ Deefholts, Margaret; Deefholts, Glenn; Acharya, Quentine (2006). The Way We Were: Anglo-Indian Cronicles. Calcutta Tiljallah Relief Inc. p. 87. ISBN 0-9754639-3-4.

159. ^ Ali 2006, pp. 163–164

160. ^ Ali 2006, p. 164

161. ^ Habib 1997, p. 96

162. ^ Chua 2007, p. 187

163. ^ Chua 2007, p. 126

164. ^ Jump up to:a b Collingham 2006, p. 30

165. ^ Jump up to:a b Collingham 2006, p. 31

166. ^ Sanghmitra. Jain Dharma ke Prabhavak Acharya. Jain Vishwa Bharati, Ladnu.

167. ^ Sen, Amartya (2005). The Argumentative Indian. Allen Lane. pp. 288–289. ISBN 0-7139-9687-0. Akbar arranged for discussions ... involving not only

mainstream Hindu and Muslim philosophers [but Jains and others] ... Arguing with Jains, Akbar would remain sceptical of their rituals, and yet become convinced by their argument for vegetarianism and end up deploring the eating of all flesh

168. ^ Truschke, Audrey. "Jains and the Mughals". JAINpedia.

169. ^ Truschke, Audrey (2012). "Setting the Record Wrong: A Sanskrit Vision of Mughal Conquests". South Asian History and Culture. 3 (3): 373. doi:10.1080/19472498.2012.693710. S2CID 145619920.

170. ^ "Ahmedabad turned Akbar veggie". The Times of India. 23 November 2009. Retrieved 23 November 2009.

171. ^ p. 137, Poetry of Kings: The Classical Hindi Literature of Mughal India by Allison Busch

172. ^ Habib, Irfan (September–October 1992). "Akbar and Technology". Social Scientist. 20 (9–10): 3–15. doi:10.2307/3517712. JSTOR 3517712.

173. ^ Richards, John F. (1996). The Mughal Empire. Cambridge University Press. p. 35. ISBN 978-0-521-56603-2.

174. ^ Jahangir (1600s). Tuzk-e-Jahangiri (Memoirs of Jahangir).

175. ^ Codrington, K. de B. (March 1943). "Portraits of Akbar, the Great Mughal (1542–1605)". The Burlington Magazine for Connoisseurs. 82 (480): 64–67. JSTOR 868499.

176. ^ Garbe, Richard von (1909). Akbar, Emperor of India. Chicago: The Open Court Publishing Company.

177. ^ Richards, John F. (1996). The Mughal Empire. Cambridge University Press. p. 15. ISBN 978-0-521-56603-2.

178. ^ Hardwar Archived 20 September 2011 at the Wayback Machine Ain-e-Akbari, by Abul Fazl 'Allami, Volume I,

A'I'N 22. The A'bda'r Kha'nah. p. 55. Translated from the original Persian, by Heinrich Blochmann and Colonel Henry Sullivan Jarrett, Asiatic society of Bengal. Calcutta, 1873–1907.

179. ^ "1200–1750". University of Hamburg. Archived from the original on 22 February 2008. Retrieved 30 May 2008.

180. ^ Jump up to:a b Sangari 2007, p. 497

181. ^ Sangari 2007, p. 475

182. ^ Jump up to:a b "Art Access: Indian, Himalayan, and Southeast Asian". artic.edu. The Art Institute of Chicago. Archived from the original on 19 September 2009. Retrieved 20 February 2010.

183. ^ Jahangir & Thackston 1999, p. 40.

184. ^ Jump up to:a b c d Burke, S. M. (1989). Akbar: The Greatest Mogul. Munshiram Manoharlal Publishers. pp. 142, 143, 144.

185. ^ Beveridge Volume II 1907, p. 88.

186. ^ Jahangir & Thackston 1999, p. 140.

187. ^ Beveridge Volume II 1907, pp. 240–243.

188. ^ Jahangir & Thackston 1999, p. 397.

189. ^ Abd-ul-Qadir bin Maluk Shah (1884). Muntakhab-ut-Tawarikh by Al-Badaoni translated from the original Persian by W.H. Lowe – Volume II. Asiatic Society of Bengal, Calcutta. pp. 59–60.

190. ^ Maulavi Abdur Rahim. Ma'asir al-Umara by Nawab Shams-ud-Daulah Shahnawaz Khan – Volume II (Persian). Asiatic Society of Bengal, Calcutta. pp. 564, 566.

191. ^ The Mertiyo Rathors of Merta, Rajasthan. Vol. II. pp. 366–367.

192. ^ Beveridge Volume II 1907, p. 352.

193. ^ Quddusi, Mohd. Ilyas (2002). Khandesh under the

Mughals, 1601–1724 A.D.: mainly based on Persian sources. Islamic Wonders Bureau. p. 4.

194. ^ Jump up to:a b "Raj+kanwari"+ A Persian historiography in India. 2003. pp. 78–79. ISBN 9788173915376.

195. ^ Fazl, Abu'l. Akbarnama. Vol. II. p. 518.

196. ^ Beveridge Volume II 1907, p. 518.

197. ^ Manchanda, Bindu. Jaisalmer: The City of Golden Sands and Strange Spirits. Jaisalmer, India. p. 24.

198. ^ Somani, Ramavallabha. History of Jaisalmer. p. 55.

199. ^ Beveridge Volume II 1907, pp. 518–519.

200. ^ Beveridge Volume II 1907, p. 283.

201. ^ The Mertiyo Rathors of Merta, Rajasthan. Vol. I. p. 4.

202. ^ The Mertiyo Rathors of Merta, Rajasthan. Vol. II. p. 362.

203. ^ Hasan Siddiqi, Mahmudul (1972). History of the Arghuns and Tarkhans of Sindh, 1507–1593: An Annotated Translation of the Relevant Parts of Mir Ma'sums Ta'rikh-i-Sindh, with an Introduction & Appendices. Institute of Sindhology, University of Sind. p. 166.

204. ^ Ahsan, Aitzaz (2005). The Indus Saga. Roli Books Private Limited. ISBN 978-9-351-94073-9.

205. ^ Akhtar, Muhammad Saleem (1983). Sindh under the Mughals: An Introduction to, translation of and commentary on the Mazhar-i Shahjahani of Yusuf Mirak (1044/1634). pp. 78, 79, 81.

206. ^ Beveridge Volume III 1907, pp. 167–168.

207. ^ Beveridge Volume III 1907, p. 278.

208. ^ Beveridge Volume III 1907, p. 295.

209. ^ Jahangir & Thackston 1999, p. 39.

210. ^ Akbarnama of Abu'l Fazl Volume III. p. 661. One of

the occurrences was the birth of Ārām Bānū Begam.* On 12 Dai, 22 December 1584, divine month, and the 19th degree of Sagittarius, and according to the calculation of the Indians, one degree and 54 minutes, that night-gleaming jewel of fortune appeared, and glorified the harem of the Shāhinshāh.

211.   ^ Beveridge Volume III 1907, p. 661.

212.   ^ Beveridge Volume III 1907, p. 958.

213.   ^ Beveridge Volume III 1907, p. 985.

214.   ^ Sreenivasan, Ramya (2006), Indrani Chatterjee; Richard M. Eaton (eds.), "Drudges, dancing girls, concubines: female slaves in Rajput polity, 1500–1850", Slavery and South Asian History, Bloomington, Indiana: Indiana University Press: 152, 159, ISBN 0-253-11671-6

215.   ^ Chandra, Satish (1993). Mughal Religious Policies, the Rajputs & the Deccan. New Delhi, India: Vikas Publishing House. pp. 17–18. ISBN 978-0-7069-6385-4.

216.   ^ "Remembering Akbar the Great: Facts about the most liberal Mughal emperor". India Today. 27 October 2016. Retrieved 31 January 2021.

217.   ^ Majumdar 1984, pp. 168–169

218.   ^ Habib 1997, p. 79

219.   ^ Majumdar 1984, p. 170

220.   ^ Meenakshi Khanna (2007). Cultural History of Medieval India. Berghahn Books. pp. 34–35. ISBN 978-81-87358-30-5. Retrieved 30 June 2013.

221.   ^ The Imperial and Asiatic Quarterly Review and Oriental and Colonial Record. Oriental Institute. 1900. pp. 158–161. Retrieved 29 June 2013.

222.   ^ Ali, Mubarak (September–October 1992). "Akbar in Pakistani Textbooks". Social Scientist. 20 (9/10): 73–76. doi:10.2307/3517719. JSTOR 3517719.

223.   ^ The Mertiyo Rathors of Merta, Rajasthan; Volume II.
         p. 51.

Bibliography

- Ali, M. Athar (2006). Mughal India: Studies in Polity, Ideas, Society and Culture. Oxford University Press. ISBN 978-0-19-569661-5.
- Chandra, Satish (2007). History of Medieval India. New Delhi: Orient Longman. ISBN 978-81-250-3226-7.
- Chua, Amy (2007). Day of Empire: How Hyperpowers Rise to Global Dominance – and Why They Fall. Doubleday. ISBN 978-0-385-51284-8.
- Collingham, Lizzie (2006). Curry: A Tale of Cooks and Conquerors. Oxford University Press. ISBN 978-0-19-532001-5.
- Faroqhi, Suraiya (2006). The Ottoman Empire and the World Around It. I.B. Tauris. ISBN 978-1-84511-122-9.
- Habib, Irfan (1997). Akbar and His India. New Delhi: Oxford University Press. ISBN 978-0-19-563791-5.
- Hasan, Nurul (2007). Religion, State and Society in Medieval India. New Delhi: Oxford University Press. ISBN 978-0-19-569660-8.
- Majumdar, R. C., ed. (1974). History and Culture of the Indian People. Vol. VII. Bombay: Bharatiya Vidya Bhavan.
- Majumdar, R.C. (1984). The Mughul Empire. Bombay: Bharatiya Vidya Bhavan.
- Moosvi, Shireen (2008). People, Taxation and Trade in Mughal India. New Delhi: Oxford University Press. ISBN 978-0-19-569315-7.
- Nath, R. (1982). History of Mughal Architecture. Abhinav Publications. ISBN 978-81-7017-159-1.
- Sangari, Kumkum (2007). "Akbar: The Name of a

Conjuncture". In Grewal, J.S. (ed.). The State and Society in Medieval India. New Delhi: Oxford University Press. pp. 475–501. ISBN 978-0-19-566720-2.

- Sarkar, Jadunath (1984). A History of Jaipur. New Delhi: Orient Longman. ISBN 81-250-0333-9.
- Smith, Vincent Arthur (1917). Akbar the Great Mogul, 1542–1605. Oxford at The Clarendon Press.
- Smith, Vincent A. (2002). The Oxford History of India. Oxford University Press. ISBN 978-0-19-561297-4.
- Beveridge, Henry (1907). Akbarnama of Abu'l-Fazl ibn Mubarak – Volume II. Asiatic Society, Calcutta.
- Beveridge, Henry (1907). Akbarnama of Abu'l-Fazl ibn Mubarak – Volume III. Asiatic Society, Calcutta.
- Jahangir, Emperor; Thackston, Wheeler McIntosh (1999). The Jahangirnama : memoirs of Jahangir, Emperor of India. Washington, D.C.: Freer Gallery of Art, Arthur M. Sackler Gallery, Smithsonian Institution; New York: Oxford University Press. pp. 168, 316. ISBN 978-0-19-512718-8.
- Wiegand, Wayne A.; Davis, Jr., Donald G., eds. (1994). "India". Encyclopedia of Library History. Garland Publishing, Inc. ISBN 0-8240-5787-2.